95 "Precious Promises"
—II Peter 1:4

Robert L. Sumner

Biblical Evangelism Press
Brownsburg, Indiana 46112

Copyright © 1978
BIBLICAL EVANGELISM
ISBN: 0-914012-18-5

Printed in the United States of America

Dedication

These "Precious Promises" Are
Joyfully Dedicated to
My "Precious" Grandchildren

Randy Lee Sumner
Robin Michelle Sumner

Heather LeAnn Phipps
Shannon Lynne Phipps

David Alan Purvis
Kimberly Anne Purvis

AUTHOR'S PREFACE

How sweet are God's wonderful promises, scattered in such abundance throughout His blessed Word! The huge unabridged Random House Dictionary of the English Language in our office defines *precious* as "of high price or great value; very valuable or costly." How fitting that the Apostle Peter, writing to those who had "obtained like precious faith" with him, enthused so excitedly about the "exceeding great and precious promises" which have been given to us in Christ Jesus (II Peter 1:1,4). The promises considered in this volume are only the tip of the iceberg; thousands more are still lying beneath the surface of the Sacred Scriptures and this study is intended only to stir the believer's enthusiasm for searching them out.

Just how many promises are there in the Word of God? Two prominent figures offered repeatedly by Bible teachers and other public speakers are 30,000 and 33,000. Just recently one Christian magazine gave the 30,000 number, probably the most popular of the two.

Simple logic should disprove such exorbitant claims in short order. The New Testament only contains 7,959 verses. While the Old Testament has nearly three times that number, 23,214, this still only makes a total of 31,173 verses for the entire Bible. It stands to reason that the Word of God does not have almost as many *(or more!)* promises as it does verses. Anyone who has waded through the seemingly endless genealogies, considered the extended historical portions, read the various poetical sections, and studied the many commands and instructions about righteous living and fruitful service would know beyond a shadow of doubt that a promise for every verse is totally and completely unrealistic.

Dr. Keith L. Brooks, late editor of the greatly missed *Prophecy* magazine, troubled by the many exaggerated claims, set out to count them. He discovered 661 verses containing promises in the New Testament and 1,298 verses with promises in the Old. He broke them down:

Promises from God to man: 3,827 (1,018 in the New Testament; 2,809 in the Old).

Promises from man to man: 173 (10 in the New Testament; 163 in the Old).

Promises from man to God: 180 (8 in the New Testament; 172 in the Old).

Promises from Satan to Jesus: 3 (New Testament).

Promises from the Father to the Son: 3 (New Testament).

In the 47 hours (40 sittings) it took him to complete his count, he found a grand total of 4,186.

Dr. Herbert Lockyer, in his excellent volume, *All the Promises of the Bible,* refers to the research of a Canadian schoolteacher, Everet R. Storms of Kitchener. He purported to find:

Promises from God to man: 7,487.

Promises from the Father to the Son: 2.

Promises from man to man: 991.

Promises from man to God: 290.

Promises made by angels: 21.

Promise made by a man to an angel: 1.

Promises from an evil spirit to the Lord: 2.

Promises from Satan: 9.

This is a grand total, according to Storms' research, of 8,810. (The figures given above actually come only to 8,803; Lockyer does not explain the discrepency.)

Obviously, the difference between Brooks' total and the one offered by Storms emphasizes the conclusion that a promise, like beauty, is in the eye of the beholder. Too, both men based their figures on a single scanning, a fact admittedly neither scientific nor conducive to accuracy. Suffice it to say, while neither figure approaches the mystical 30,000 or 33,000 given by so many speakers who have not troubled themselves with personal investigation, there are enough of God's "exceeding great and precious promises" to meet every facet of the believer's walk, work and warfare.

The evaluations of God's promises in this volume were prepared over a span of several years. Most were published, one by one and a month at a time, in a magazine the writer edits, THE BIBLICAL EVANGELIST, appearing in the column, " 'Precious Promises' Powerhouse." Another eight or ten were prepared especially for this book.

May every reader be encouraged to *search out* and *claim* additional promises personally, writing the *proof* of those promises in his or her own life. Remember, "They that trust in the Lord shall be as mount Zion, which cannot be removed, but abideth for ever" (Psalm 125:1). ". . .*the word of the Lord is tried*. . ." (Psalm 18:30).

1. THE PROMISE: *"Wherefore the Lord God of Israel saith, I said indeed that thy house, and the house of thy father, should walk before me for ever: but now the Lord saith, Be it far from me; FOR THEM THAT HONOUR ME I WILL HONOUR, and they that despise me shall be lightly esteemed"* (I Samuel 2:30).

2. THE POINT: While these words of Jehovah were given to Eli in a setting of warning and chastening because of his failure with his sons, Hophni and Phinehas, this precious gem that those who honor the Lord will be honored by Him is nonetheless true. Those who step out by faith to put God first, even in the midst of circumstances looking like inevitable loss, will be vindicated by God in His own time.

3. THE PROOF: The life of the multi-millionaire industrialist Robert Gilmour LeTourneau, makes fascinating reading. Lost and undone the first 16 years of his life, he was soundly converted in a revival meeting. This was followed by a second 16-year span spent in living a selfish, carnal, fruitless Christian life. It, too, was broken during a revival crusade which saw him kneeling at an old-fashioned altar and crying, "Lord, if You will give me a victorious Christian life and put the love in my heart that I know ought to be there and fill me with Your Spirit so that I can witness for You, I'll do whatever you ask me to do from this day on." This was followed by a conviction to do his best as "God's businessman."

Physical deliverances—such as when he was attacked by a herd of wild steers, when a by-stander threw a bucket of gasoline instead of water on a fire which broke out while he was working on a car, and the broken neck he received when a race car he was driving crashed through a fence—in LeTourneau's life were tame when compared to some of the spiritual victories won after his yielding to Christ.

On one occasion he had contracted for a million-dollar highway to Boulder Dam in Nevada and a half-million-dollar contract for the Orange County Dam in Southern California. The highway was handled first and unforeseen difficulties resulted in a net loss of about $100,000. This, in turn, meant LeTourneau would have to have outside financial help to swing the dam deal. A San Francisco bonding company agreed to put up the money if "R. G." would allow its overseer to superintend the work. He consented, reluctantly.

Further complications arose when a state inspector first refused to allow the start of the work so near the rainy season (and a wait until Spring would have put the struggling company under financially), then agreed to permit it if LeTourneau could build the 400,000 cubic yards needed for the base of the dam within one month. Although this was twice the cubic yards planned for the first month, the small crew not only *tackled* the project but *did* it, working around the clock, day and night.

Since LeTourneau was not in the habit of working his men on Sunday, he then approached the overseer about a 6-day work week. He was not only refused the request, but the overseer told him that if he tried it, the bonding company would take over the project and he would lose everything.

Feeling he should obey God rather than men, LeTourneau went to his foremen on Saturday night and told them to tell the men there would be no Sunday work. The next morning only the overseer and his assistant showed up. Things started popping fast! The head man at the bonding company in San Francisco got "R. G." on the phone and issued an ultimatum: "Work on Sunday or we take over the project!" LeTourneau replied: "I cannot change my decision. You can take everything I have except my wife and children."

Three days later the head of the bonding company flew in, walked up to LeTourneau, put out his hand and said, "Go ahead. I will stand behind you." Without the Sunday work the job was completed on time and the profits put the company back on its feet. God had honored LeTourneau for honoring Him!

4. THE POEM:

>Jesus, Thou has bought us, not with gold or gem,
>But with Thine own life blood, for Thy diadem;
>With Thy blessing filling each who comes to Thee,
>Thou hast made us willing, Thou hast made us free.
>By Thy grand redemption, by Thy grace divine,
>We are on the Lord's side—Savior, we are Thine!
>
>Fierce may be the conflict, strong may be the foe,
>But the King's own army none can overthrow:
>Round His standard ranging, vict'ry to secure;
>For His truth unchanging makes the triumph sure.
>Joyfully enlisting, by Thy grace divine,
>We are on the Lord's side—Savior, we are Thine!
>
>—*Frances Ridley Havergal* (1836-1879)

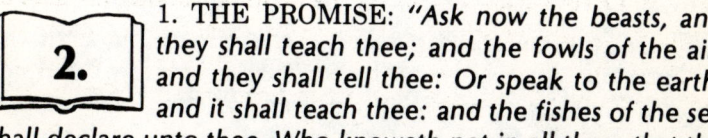

1. THE PROMISE: *"Ask now the beasts, and they shall teach thee; and the fowls of the air, and they shall tell thee: Or speak to the earth, and it shall teach thee: and the fishes of the sea shall declare unto thee. Who knoweth not in all these that the hand of the Lord hath wrought this? In whose hand is the soul of every living thing, and the breath of all mankind"* (Job 12:7-10).

2. THE POINT: Our God Jehovah holds the whole world in His hand—the beast of the field, the fowl of the sky, the fish of the sea and man himself—and He can make one or all do His bidding at any time He so desires.

3. THE PROOF: Billy Bray, the ex-drunken miner, felt led of God to build a chapel in the area of Cornwall County, England, where he lived. After his mother had donated a piece of land for the building, Billy ran into all kinds of local opposition. Some tried to get the preachers against him, others openly opposed him, some suggested different locations for the chapel, and some promised to help, then refused. Undaunted, the man with the

reputation for "always rejoicing" went on with the work.

Money came in to provide materials in a manner that could only be described as miraculous. After recounting several such incidents, Billy went on to say:

"After that I wanted timber for the door and windows and forms. A mine had lately stopped; and they were selling off the timber. There was a bargain in timber for one pound six shillings; but I had not money to buy it. To a friend who asked me whether I had been to the mine, and bought any timber, I said I had not, because I had no money. Then he gave me one pound, and with that and some other sums the Lord sent me from other places, I was able to buy what I wanted.

"As the timber had to be brought home to the dear Lord's house, I wanted a horse and cart. One of our neighbors had a horse, but he said she would not draw anything. I asked him to lend her to me. He told me I might have her, but she would not draw.

"I took the mare and put her in the cart and brought the timber home. I never saw a better horse in my life; I did not touch her with whip or stick, though we had steep hills to come up over. When I took back the mare, and told my neighbor, 'I never had a better mare,' he said, 'I never saw such a thing; she will not draw with any one else.'

"That mare was working that day for a very strong company—Father, Son and Holy Ghost—whom horses, angels, men, and devils must obey. If there had been no one there more powerful than Billy Bray, she would have been as bad with him as with anybody else. But, bless and praise the name of the dear Lord! He said, 'The horse shall work, for the timber is to seat My house'; and what the dear Lord says shall be obeyed.

"I went on and finished the chapel. . . ."

4. THE POEM:

> And lo! all round us His bright servants stand;
> Events, His duteous ministers and wise,
> With frowning brows, perhaps, for their disguise,

But with such wells of love in their deep eyes,
And such strong rescue hidden in their hands!

And our lives may in glory move along;
First holy white, and then all good, and fair
For our dear Lord to see,—the meanest thong
Of all that whips us, welcome,—and the air
We breathe, self-shaped into a natural song.

—*Henry Septimus Sutton*

1. THE PROMISE: *"Out of the mouth of babes and sucklings hast thou ordained strength because of thine enemies, that thou mightest still the enemy and the avenger"* (Psalm 8:2).

2. THE POINT: God is not limited in His use of human instruments. He is as capable of using an innocent child to reach the heart of a rebellious enemy as He is a Spurgeon, a Torrey, or a Billy Sunday. The Saviour reminded His enemies of this promise when they objected to the adoration of the Son of God by the little children (Matthew 21:15,16).

3. THE PROOF: A missionary in Cincinnati, Ohio, tells this true story:

"A dear, pious lady had long been praying for the conversion of her husband. She was in the habit of praying that God might, in His own good time, bring about a change of heart and mind, using whatever means He chose.

"On a certain evening, when she had gone to the house of worship, her husband was at home busily engaged in reading his paper, their little daughter seated on his knee. Presently the little child said, 'Papa, why do you not talk to me about Jesus, as Mama does?'

"He made no reply, but dropped the paper he was reading. The simple inquiry of his child, like an arrow, pierced his heart and conscience. He sat for a moment, quiet and speechless. The question was repeated, 'Papa, why don't you tell me about Jesus, like Mama does?'

"Putting the child down, he now called the servant girl and told her to put Mamie to bed, as he wanted to go to church to meet his wife. He very seldom came to the house of prayer, and his visit that night surprised many. As the service was nearing the close, the minister said, 'If any desire the prayers of the church for the salvation of their souls, let them rise to their feet.'

"Without a moment's delay he stood up, while his dear wife bowed down and wept. There were also many others weeping for joy to see this man finally yielding to God. The congregation earnestly prayed for his conversion and the prayers were answered. Before he left the house he rejoiced in the God of his salvation.

"The joy of his wife was great. On going home she inquired, 'How was it you came to the meeting tonight?' He said, 'I was driven to go, Mamie's question troubled me so much. I could not talk about Jesus, for I did not love Him. But I now know Him, and love Him, and shall serve Him all my life.' "

The husband truly became a devoted Christian, eventually serving in the capacity of Sunday school superintendent. And his daughter, Mamie, became one of the teachers!

4. THE POEM:

>I have not much to offer
> To Christ, my Lord and King;
>No wealth, no might, no wisdom,
> No noble gift to bring.
>"Five loaves and two small fishes?"
> But what alas are they
>Among the throngs of hungry
> Who crowd life's troubled way?
>"Five loaves and two small fishes?"
> Not much, dear heart, 'tis true;
>But yield them to the Master,
> And see what He can do!
>Placed in His hands of mercy,

> Thy little will be much.
> 'Tis not thy gift that matters,
> But His almighty touch!¹
> —*Avis Marguerite Burgeson Christiansen*

©1962 by Singspiration, Inc., Grand Rapids, Michigan. All rights reserved. Used by permission.

1. THE PROMISE: *"The Lord also will be a refuge for the oppressed, a refuge in times of trouble. And they that know thy name will put their trust in thee: for thou, Lord, hast not forsaken them that seek thee"* (Psalm 9:9,10).

2. THE POINT: While every individual is periodically faced with trouble, no child of God need be swallowed up by it. Whenever those who "know Jehovah's name" flee to Him for aid, He gives them the help they need. He never forsakes them!

3. THE PROOF: "I am willing to be the *second* whom thou forsakest, but I shall *not* be the first!" Thus prayed Beate Paulus, the wife of a German clergyman who lived near the Black Forest, when faced with financial problems which had caused even her husband to despair.

Longing to give her children a good education, five of her sons were scattered in different schools in different cities when she received notices from three of the institutions that unless bills for tuition and board were settled immediately, the boys would be dismissed. Her husband, in anguish, spread out the letters on the table before her, crying: "There, look at them, and pay your debts with your faith!"

Calmly, confidently, she replied: "These accounts will be settled at an early date. He, who owns the silver and the gold, will find it an easy matter to provide these sums."

Going to her secret closet in an upper loft, she presented her case to the Lord, reminding Him that it was in His name and for His sake that she sought an education for her children and that now monies were needed for due bills. She told Him of her husband's unbelief and need of strengthened faith. She reminded Him that He had brought her back from the very gates of death, for her children's sake, and now they had additional needs. That was when she cried: "Now, O most precious Lord, do not forsake me at this juncture. I am willing to be the *second* whom Thou forsakest, but I shall *not* be the first!"

Beate Paulus continued wrestling with God through the supper hour and then all through the night. About mid-morning she appeared with her countenance beaming. As a matter of fact, so radiant was she that her young daughter rushed up, exclaiming, "Mamma, what has happened to you? Did an angel bring you the money?" She replied, "No, Dear, but it will surely come."

Almost immediately a messenger appeared, saying, "The proprietor of the inn requests to see 'Frau Pastorin,' if she can come to see him." She went at once and the innkeeper, a noble Christian gentleman, greeted her with the words: "Frau Pastorin, I am glad you have come. I have a little money in the house which I have been thinking of devoting to some good cause. Now, during the whole of last night I could not rest, thinking continually that you were in trouble. I therefore resolved that you should have the money. Here it is; take it right with you." Then he handed her three separate packages of money, saying he hoped God's blessing would rest upon the gift. When she related with what agony of heart she had been praying for hours, the innkeeper exclaimed: "How wonderful are the ways of the Lord! Now I am doubly glad that through me the Lord has answered your prayers."

You can well imagine with what joy she hurried home, reopened the letters from the three schools before her husband, laying the required sum of money upon each one, and, face radiant with joy, bubbled: "Praise God for another deliverance!" Then she added the rebuke, "Now believe that faith in God is no empty madness."

Thank God, it is not! He never forsakes those who seek Him.

4. THE POEM:

>Even as a nurse, whose child's imperfect pace
>Can hardly lead his foot from place to place,
>Leaves her fond kissing, sets him down to go,
>Nor does uphold him for a step or two;
>But when she finds that he begins to fall,
>She holds him up and kisses him withal—
>So God from man sometimes withdraws His hand
>Awhile to teach His infant faith to stand;
>But when He sees his feeble strength begin
>To fail, He gently takes him up again.
>—*Francis Quarles* (1592-1644)

5.

1. THE PROMISE: *"For the righteous Lord loveth righteousness; his countenance doth behold the upright"* (Psalm 11:7).

2. THE POINT: The very nature of God's holiness causes Him to delight in the righteousness of His servants. Not only so, but He gives special blessing for those who manifest deeds of uprightness in their lives. In fact, such acts can even reverse our own defeats.

3. THE PROOF: The noted English evangelist, Henry Moorhouse, whose preaching that God loved even the worst of sinners revolutionized the ministry of Dwight L. Moody, had an only child, Minnie, who was paralyzed. He tells how, on one occasion, he "got downhearted, cloudy and dark. It was a very miserable day; at least, I was miserable. I do not think Christians ought to be miserable, no matter what kind of days there are. But so it was with me.

"It was Christmas Eve and there was a thick fog all over Manchester, where I was; and the miserable sleety rain was coming down. I looked at my watch, and it was about eight o'clock.

Four miles away there was a little cottage, with a bright fire and a nice cup of tea ready for me. I thought to myself, 'I will get right home and make myself comfortable.' But at the moment I thought of a little child two miles away. There were no 'busses and no trams—I should have to trudge all the way; and it was Christmas Eve.

"I began to think, 'Well now, little girls will want to have a doll tomorrow; I wonder if anybody has taken anything to this little child. It will be eleven o'clock before I get home if I go; and what will my wife say to my going home so late? And I will have to walk through the rain, and the slush, and the fog.' Something whispered, 'I would not do it if I were you.'

"But then another thought came: 'Suppose that child were your little Minnie, and there was no one to give her anything.' I went into a toy shop, bought a doll for a few pence, and started off through the cold and the wet. By and by I came to a cellar, where this child lived with her mother and little brother. I knocked at the door and a voice said, 'Come in.' I put my thumb on the latch and went inside.

"There was a miserable little bit of fire burning, and no candle. By the light of the fire I saw the little boy sitting on one side and lying on the bed there was the little girl, about nine years old. She was suffering from a terrible disease; she was going to have her little leg taken off in a few weeks.

"She said to me, 'I am so glad you could come; nobody has been to see us; and mother has gone to see if she could get anything to do, and get some money to buy the Christmas dinner with.'

"I said, 'I have come to give you a doll,' and I gave it to her. The little thing looked at it; then she put her hand into the bed and took out some old rags. She said, 'I have been trying to make a doll myself, but I have got a real one now.' She took the doll I gave her, and kissed it.

"In a moment the darkness had gone from my spirit; the cold, chilly feeling had disappeared; and I was as happy as ever I could be. I would not have missed taking that doll, that only cost threepence or fourpence, for a five-pound note. How glad it had made me! And the next day the happiness I had in seeing my own little girl was ten times more, because I knew another little girl was made happy, too."

4. THE POEM:

> **The heart grows rich in giving,**
> **All its wealth is living grain,**
> **Seeds, which mildew in the garden,**
> **Scattered, fill with gold the plain.**
>
> **Is thy burden hard and heavy?**
> **Do thy steps drag wearily?**
> **Help to bear thy brother's burden—**
> **God will bear both it and thee.**

6.

1. THE PROMISE: *"I will bless the Lord, who hath given me counsel: my reins also instruct me in the night seasons"* (Psalm 16:7).

2. THE POINT: Ofttimes Christians, in their extremities, do not know which way to turn. Trying to find their way out, sometimes they find their own plans blocked and some other door, previously unknown, is opened which proves far more beneficial. This counsel is especially precious in the night seasons of testing.

3. THE PROOF: When the noted author, Paul Hutchens, was just starting out in his early days of evangelism, he had not a few "extenuating financial circumstances." On one occasion he was "marking time" in Iowa, waiting for a meeting in Georgia, still two weeks distant, when his money ran out.

Walking in the country, trying to get temporary employment as a farm hand during the harvest season, the penniless preacher had made a fruitless trip into a field and experienced another job "turn down." When he crawled back through the barbed-wire fence, he heard the spine chilling sound of trousers being ripped!

Insult had been added to injury!

Talk about being discouraged! He shuffled along, head down, when all of a sudden he spotted a shiny object in the dust. Grabbing what turned out to be a thin dime, the temporarily-revived job seeker headed for a restaurant to break an unwilling fast with a 10¢ sandwich. While eating the lunch, he made inquiries about work and learned of a lady who needed a lawn mowed. Believe it or not, he got a silver dollar in those depression days for "a few minutes' work."

Then someone told him of a Baptist Camp nearby where dishwashers were needed in exchange for room and board. Hutchens was hired, had plenty of tasty and nourishing food to eat, a roof over his head, fellowship with young people his own age, learned lessons from the conference sessions (he is still preaching parts of one sermon he picked up there), and otherwise profited immensely in a number of ways.

As he summed it up: "Just how the dime in the road shared in what happened. . .I'm not quite sure, but I am sure it would have been a missing of the Lord's will for me to have found a week's work on a farm."

4. THE POEM:

>I do not ask, O Lord, that life may be
>A pleasant road;
>I do not ask that Thou wouldst take from me
>Aught of its load;
>I do not ask that flowers should always spring
>Beneath my feet;
>I know too well the poison and the sting
>Of things too sweet.
>
>For one thing only, Lord, dear Lord, I plead—
>Lead me aright,
>Though strength should falter, and though heart should bleed,
>Through Peace to Light.
>I do not ask, O Lord, that Thou shouldst shed
>Full radiance here;

Give but a ray of peace, that I may tread
   Without a fear.

I do not ask my cross to understand,
   My way to see;
Better in darkness just to feel Thy hand
   And follow Thee.
Joy is like restless day; but peace divine
   Like quiet night;
Lead me, O Lord, till perfect day shall shine,
   Through Peace to Light.

—*Adelaide Anne Proctor* (1825-1864)

7.

1. THE PROMISE: *"The heavens declare the glory of God; and the firmament sheweth his handywork. Day unto day uttereth speech, and night unto night sheweth knowledge. There is no speech nor language, where their voice is not heard. Their line is gone out through all the earth, and their words to the end of the world. . . .The law of the Lord is perfect, converting the soul: the testimony of the Lord is sure, making wise the simple. The statutes of the Lord are right, rejoicing the heart: the commandment of the Lord is pure, enlightening the eyes. The fear of the Lord is clean, enduring for ever: the judgments of the Lord are true and righteous altogether. More to be desired are they than gold, yea, than much fine gold: sweeter also than honey and the honeycomb. Moreover by them is thy servant warned: and in keeping of them there is great reward"* (Psalm 19:1-4b, 7-11).

2. THE POINT: The omnipotent God whose glory is seen so succinctly in creation—with its universal testimony understood in every language—may be counted on to fulfill any declaration of His Word, no matter whether it pertains to the conversion of the soul, the commandments of consecration, or some other es-

sential in our relationship to Him.

3. THE PROOF: The noted revivalist of yesteryear, Billy Sunday, in his famous sermon, "The Faultless Christ," made the following observation:

"I went to visit the Waltham watchworks. Down in the basement they have what they call the master clock. It is surrounded by several thicknesses of wall. It is kept at a normal temperature the year around.

"They have a gas arrangement in there, a thermostat that is automatically lighted by electricity. When the temperature reaches a certain degree, the light will go on, and when it gets to a certain degree, it will go out.

"Now there is the clock resting upon a foundation that goes down, my friends, below the river. Then attached to it, they have a little machine with a cylinder. On that is a piece of paper, and fastened on that is a fountain pen. As the clock ticks, that fountain pen makes a little mark on this cylinder of paper.

"Out yonder stands an observatory, one of the finest in the United States, resting upon a foundation that goes fifty feet below the bed of the river. There sit expert men, astronomers with a large telescope, and they sit there and watch the stars. As the stars go by, they push a button and it records it with a fountain pen on another cylinder down in the basement near this great master clock.

"Then every twenty-four hours they compare these two cylinders. If the one made by the tick of the clock doesn't harmonize with the cylinder made by the astronomers, then the clock is wrong. The stars are never wrong!

"Say, let me tell you something. Do you regulate your life by the Bible? God is never wrong. You are wrong! You adjust yourself and see what He will do."[1]

4. THE POEM:

    We search the world for truth; we cull
    The good, the pure, the beautiful
    From graven stone and written scroll,

From all old flower-fields of the soul.
And we are seekers of the best;
We come back laden from our quest,
To find what all the sages said,
Is in the Book our mothers read.
—*John Greenleaf Whittier* (1807-1892)

[1] THE BEST OF BILLY SUNDAY, Compiled and edited by John R. Rice. Copyright 1965 by Sword of the Lord Publishers, Murfreesboro, Tennessee. Used by permission.

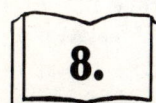

1. THE PROMISE: *"Yea, though I walk through the valley of the shadow of death, I will fear no evil: for thou art with me; thy rod and thy staff they comfort me"* (Psalm 23:4).

2. THE POINT: Death should hold no fear for the child of God! Described for him as only a "shadow," he has the sweet assurance of his blessed Redeemer's presence and comfort to usher him safely into the Land that is fairer than day. In a very real sense, death is not dying!

3. THE PROOF: One of the simplest of all God's wonderful promises to illustrate, consider the following testimonies of dying saints:

The famous evangelist, Dwight Lyman Moody, speaking in slow and measured words, said: "Earth recedes; Heaven opens before me. . .No, this is no dream, Will. It is beautiful. It is like a trance. If this is death, it is sweet. There is no valley here. God is calling me and I must go. . .This is my triumph; this is my coronation day! I have been looking forward to it for years."

John Bunyan, author of the immortal *Pilgrim's Progress,* declared: "Weep not for me, but for yourselves. I go to the Father of our Lord Jesus Christ, who will, through the mediation of His blessed Son, receive me, though a sinner, where I hope we shall meet to sing the new song, and remain everlastingly happy, world without end."

The noted John Calvin, revered father of the Presbyterians, exclaimed: "Thou Lord, bruisest me, but I am abundantly satisfied, since it is from Thy hand." And the founder of Methodism, John Wesley, declared: "The best of all is, God is with us."

Martin Luther testified: "Our God is the God from whom cometh salvation. God is the Lord by whom we escape death! Into Thy hands I commit my spirit: God of truth, Thou hast redeemed me!"

The man who wrote the famous hymn, *Rock of Ages,* Augustus Montague Toplady, enthused: "The Celestial City rises full in sight, the sense of interest in the covenant of grace becomes clearer and brighter. The Book of Life is opened to the eye of assurance, the Holy Spirit more feelingly applies the blood of sprinkling, and warms the soul with that robe of righteousness which Jesus wrought."

4. THE POEM:

>Why should I be afraid?
>　It is not death to die.
>'Tis but a step to glory
>　And a mansion in the sky.
>
>How can I be afraid?
>　The Lord is with me still,
>And loves me as He did that day
>　He died upon the hill.
>
>Afraid? Of what? no night's so dark
>　It can His glory dim!
>Afraid? Oh, no! Though Jordan roar
>　I cross—dryshod—with Him.
>
>　　　　　*—Marian N. Daunecker*

9. 1. THE PROMISE: *"When thou saidst, Seek ye my face; my heart said unto thee, Thy face, Lord, will I seek. Hide not thy face far from me; put not thy servant away in anger: thou hast been my help; leave me not, neither forsake me, O God of my salvation. When my father and my mother forsake me, then the Lord will take me up"* (Psalm 27:8-10).

2. THE POINT: One who seeks the face of God, who earnestly sets out to put Him first in all things and serve Him faithfully, can expect God to wonderfully help and deliver him in times of distress and personal need. This is especially true in troubles brought about when loved ones have forsaken the child of God because of his dedication to the cause of Christ.

3. THE PROOF: Approximately a century ago a preacher by the name of John Boyd wrote the following in the *New York Witness*: "A young German lady, a native of Baden, consecrated her life to the Savior. Her father, who was an infidel, was exasperated by the change which came over the life of his daughter and drove her from his home, threatening her with disinheritance. She had heard of opportunities for Christian work in New York and was assisted financially in reaching our city through the kindness of an uncle.

"When she arrived here she was ignorant of the language and had no friends. Her money soon gave out and the poor girl was at her wits' end to know what to do. It was in this extremity that she betook herself to prayer and fasting, and agonized with God during one whole night.

"That same night her infidel father in Baden was visited by the Holy Spirit with conviction. His conscience was alarmed. He could find no rest. He awoke his wife and told her of his disquietude concerning their absent child. It was revealed to him that their daughter, who was in a far-off land, was in deep suffering and want. He told his wife that he must send a draft at once to Sophie, and though knowing nobody in New York with whom he could communicate, he had heard of a certain German newspaper, and he would immediately communicate with that paper by cablegram and letter.

"A few days after the young German girl had spent that memorable night in prayer for deliverance, as she was passing along one of the public thoroughfares of the city, she saw a soiled newspaper that had been blown about the street. She picked it up and noticed it was a German daily. A second glance revealed a notice which had direct reference to herself.

"It read as follows: 'If Miss _____, of Baden, who lately left her home for New York will call at the office of this paper, she will hear of something to her benefit,' etc. The young lady hastened with beating heart and flushed face to the office and there, to her surprise, found a letter of extraordinary affection and devotion from her father, and all the money she could possibly need for many days to come.

"The writer saw and conversed with the subject of the above sketch last night at an evangelistic meeting; and, though speaking the English language imperfectly, she is, notwithstanding, used of God in bringing many souls to the Savior. Her heart is filled with His praise and her face shines with His love."

4. THE POEM:

> **Then a voice within his breast**
> **Whispered audible and clear,**
> **As if to the outward ear,**
> **"Do thy duty, that is best,**
> **Leave unto thy Lord the rest."**
>
> *—Henry Wadsworth Longfellow (1807-1882)*

1. THE PROMISE: *"The Lord bringeth the counsel of the heathen to nought: he maketh the devices of the people of none effect"* (Psalm 33:10).

2. THE POINT: Man proposes; God disposes. All of the combined wealth, wisdom, power and prestige of the world and its worldlings are meaningless molecules before God's almighty sovereignty. He is able to withstand the most carefully planned assaults, then turn them into triumphs for His glory.

3. THE PROOF: One of the most familiar and oft-told Voltaire stories relates to his boast that the Bible would be an outmoded and forgotten book, found only in museums, within one hundred years. When the century had passed, not only had the prophecy failed and the Word of God was enjoying even greater circulation than when the threat was uttered, but the very house where the French atheist lived was now owned by the Geneva Bible Society and copies of the Sacred Scripture were stacked floor-to-ceiling in almost every room, awaiting distribution to eager readers. Not long ago, when the Earl of Derby's library was being auctioned off, a complete ninety-two volume set of Voltaire's works sold for two dollars!

Not so well known, however, is a similar story about another hater of our Lord and what happened to his home. Back in the days of the China Inland Mission, dedicated servants of our Lord pressed into the interior with His Truth until stations had been established in every province but Hunan. No "foreign devil" was permitted within its borders and, despite heroic efforts by some of God's choicest saints, the doors of Hunan stayed securely shut.

A major portion of the problem was in the person of Cheo-Han, a dedicated national who lived in Changsha, the capital of Hunan, and who kept a steady flow of anti-foreign, anti-Christian literature coming from presses in his home. Cheo-Han made large colored posters, printed from wooden blocks, which falsely accused missionaries of such atrocities as kidnaping children, then cutting out hearts and eyes to make medicine for missionary doctors. Since the Chinese ideographs for Lord and hog are much alike in sound, many of his posters would picture a hog hanging on a cross, with "foreign devils" bowing down before it in worship, while Chinese soldiers jammed spears and shot arrows into them.

Meanwhile, believers all across China—as well as many in other parts of the world—sent a wave of intercession to the Throne of Grace, crying, "O Lord, open Hunan to the Gospel of Christ!" God intervened. The Chinese authorities arrested Cheo-Han as a menace to international relations and he was sent to prison. His printing presses were confiscated, the wooden blocks with which he made his posters were burned, and his house became an American Bible Society warehouse with copies of the Word of God stacked from floor-to-ceiling in almost every room!

How frequently feeble man provides Jehovah with entertainment. As the psalmist said: "He that sitteth in the heavens shall laugh: the Lord shall have them in derision" (Psalm 2:4).

4. THE POEM:

> The Bible stands like a rock undaunted
>   'Mid the raging storms of time;
> Its pages burn with truth eternal,
>   And they glow with a light sublime.
>
> The Bible stands like a mountain tow'ring
>   Far above the works of men;
> Its truth by none ever was refuted,
>   And destroy it they never can.
>
> The Bible stands, and it will forever
>   When the world has passed away;
> By inspiration it has been given—
>   All its precepts I'll obey.
>
> The Bible stands ev'ry test we give it
>   For its Author is divine;
> By grace alone I expect to live it
>   And to prove it and make it mine.
>
> The Bible stands tho' the hills may tumble,
>   It will firmly stand when the earth shall crumble;
> I will plant my feet on its firm foundation,
>   For the Bible stands.[1]

—Halder Lillenas (1885-1959)

[1] Copyright 1917, Renewal 1945 by H. Lillenas, Assigned to Hope Publishing Co., Carol Stream, Illinois. All rights reserved. Used by permission.

11.

1. THE PROMISE: *"The eyes of the Lord are upon the righteous, and his ears are open unto their cry"* (Psalm 34:15).

2. THE POINT: Godly people have an access to the Lord which is denied the unconverted. His eyes are upon them, in the sense of favor, and He is always eager and anxious to both hear and answer their petitions.

3. THE PROOF: When A. C. Dixon was pastoring two small churches during the year between his college and seminary studies, he was invited to speak on a Sunday afternoon at a schoolhouse two miles from one of his charges. The weather was so bad that day he decided not to keep the appointment and had started for home when a young woman in a buggy caught up with him and said her father had sent her to plead with the preacher to come for the service in spite of the conditions. Reluctantly he went.

Only seven men were present and his first impression was that "it was hardly worth while to preach a regular sermon" to a congregation of such tiny size. His biographer goes on to quote him:

"But I repented of that, and gave the best I had. The dew of Heaven was upon us. We were conscious of God's presence, and two of the men expressed a desire to be saved. An old farmer arose and said: 'My young brother, God is working in our midst. Will you not preach tonight? The clouds are clearing away, and we will go out and tell the people about it.' I consented, though to stay that night in Mayesville rather upset my plans for the following day.

"There were six or seven enquirers and two or three decisions for Christ. The old farmer insisted that I should preach next day. Again I consented, and remained there, preaching in the old schoolhouse and the grove, day and night, for two weeks. There were over seventy conversions, and I baptized about forty new members of the Bear Marsh Church. I could not quite explain it. No one seemed to be expecting a revival or praying for it. I was surprised, and evidently the old farmer was surprised. But the last day of the meetings solved the mystery.

"As I came down the steps of the roughly constructed platform from which I had been preaching in the open air, a plainly dressed, grey-haired, motherly woman grasped my hand and said: 'This is my home, though I spend most of my time teaching school sixty miles from here; but when my niece wrote me that you would preach in the schoolhouse on Sunday afternoon, I said to myself, "I will pray every minute he preaches that God may save my friends." And, Sir, I have come up to see what God has been doing. All of those you baptized this morning were my neighbors, and among them were my brother, nephew and niece!' "

The mightly awakening in that country community was the direct answer to a righteous woman's petitions.

4. THE POEM:

>Teach me to pray, Lord, teach me to pray;
>This is my heart cry day unto day;
>I long to know Thy will and Thy way;
>Teach me pray, Lord, teach me to pray.
>
>Power in prayer, Lord, power in prayer,
>Here 'mid earth's sin and sorrow and care;
>Men lost and dying, souls in despair;
>O give me power, power in prayer!
>
>Teach me to pray, Lord, teach me to pray;
>Thou art my Pattern, day unto day;
>Thou art my Surety, now and for aye;
>Teach me to pray, Lord, teach me to pray.[1]
>
>—*Albert Simpson Reitz* (1879-1966)

[1] Copyright 1925 A. S. Reitz, Renewal 1953 Broadman Press, Nashville, Tennessee. All rights reserved. Used by permission.

12.

1. THE PROMISE: *"Trust in the Lord, and do good; so shalt thou dwell in the land, and verily thou shalt be fed"* (Psalm 37:3).

2. THE POINT: Faith and works, for the Christian, go hand-in-hand with blessing. The child of God who obediently serves the Lord and is willing to walk by faith will find his needs amply met by the Great Provider.

3. THE PROOF: The noted evangelist of the early 19th century, Charles G. Finney, tells of a remarkable Christian woman he met in Syracuse, New York, whom everyone called "Mother Austin." She was uneducated, reared in a family atmosphere of obvious social lack, very poor, but manifesting the greatest faith, in simplicity, he said he had ever witnessed.

In his *Autobiography*, Finney wrote: "A great many facts were related to me respecting her that showed her trust in God, and in what a remarkable manner God provided for her wants from day to day. She said to me on one occasion, 'Mr. Finney, it is impossible for me to suffer for any of the necessaries of life, because God has said to me, "Trust in the Lord and do good; so shalt thou dwell in the land, and verily thou shalt be fed."'

"She related to me many facts in her history, and many facts were related to me by others, illustrative of the power of her faith. One Saturday evening, she said, a friend of hers, but an impenitent man, called to see her, and after conversing awhile, offered her a five-dollar bill. She said she felt an inward admonition not to take it, feeling that it would be an act of self-righteousness on the part of the man, and might do him more harm than it would do her good. She, therefore, declined to take it, and he went away. She told me she had just wood and food enough in the house to last over Sunday, and that was all; that she had no means whatsoever of obtaining any more. Still she was not at all afraid to trust God in these circumstances, as she had done for so many years.

"On that Sunday morning there came a violent snowstorm. On Monday morning, the snow was several feet deep and the streets so blocked up that there was no getting out without clearing the way. She had a young son who lived with her, the two composing the whole family. They arose in the morning and found themselves snowed in on every side. They made out to muster fuel enough for a little fire, and soon the boy began to inquire what they should have for breakfast. She said, 'I do not know, my son; but the Lord will provide.'

"She looked out, and saw that nobody could pass the streets. The lad began to weep bitterly and concluded that they should freeze and starve to death. However, she said she went on and made such preparations as she would to provide for breakfast, if any should come. I think she told me she set her table and made arrangements for the meal, believing that something would come in due season.

"Very soon she heard a loud talking in the street. Going to the window to see what it was, she saw a man in a single sleigh, and some men with him shoveling the snow so that the horse could get through. Up they came to her door, and, behold, they had brought her plenty of fuel and provisions, every thing to make her comfortable for several days!

"But time would fail me to relate the instances in which she was helped in a manner as striking as this. Indeed, it was notorious through the city, so far as I could learn, that Mother Austin's faith was like a bank; and that she never suffered for want of the necessaries of life, because she drew on God."

4. THE POEM:

> The child leans on its parent's breast,
> Leaves there its cares, and is at rest;
> The bird sits singing by its nest,
>   And tells aloud
> His trust in God, and so is blest
>   'Neath every cloud.
> He hath no store, he sows no seed,
> Yet sings aloud, and doth not need,
> By flowing streams or grassy mead,
>   He sings to shame
> Men, who forget, in fear of need,
>   A Father's name.

> The heart that trusts forever sings,
> And feels as light as it had wings;
> A well of peace within it springs;
>   Come good or ill,
> Whate'er today, tomorrow, brings,
>   It is His will!
>
> —*Isaac Williams* (1802-1865)

13.

1. THE PROMISE: *"The steps of a good man are ordered by the Lord: and he delighteth in his way"* (Psalm 37:23).

2. THE POINT: Any individual who sincerely desires the will of God fulfilled in his life will find God blocking some doors and opening others as He performs the delicate task of placing His man in the position of His choice. And divine direction is always delightful!

3. THE PROOF: David Livingstone, born the first time on March 19, 1813, went to work in the cotton mills from 6 a.m. to 8 p.m. when he was only 10 years of age. At first rebuffing the claims of Christ because he thought it would mean giving up his beloved interest in science, he was converted through reading "The Philosophy of Religion" and "The Philosophy of a Future State" by Thomas Dick, and discovering that *true* science and *true* religion are perfectly compatible.

He joined a local missionary society and learned of many missionaries, such as Henry Martyn. The one who impressed him most, however, was a medical missionary to China, Charles Gutzlaff, and he determined to go himself to that land as a medical missionary. As he later wrote, "from this time my efforts were constantly devoted toward this object without any fluctuation."

At the age of 25, he applied to the London Missionary Society and was accepted as a candidate for China. Within two years he had obtained his medical degree and was ready to sail for China, the land of *his* choice. However, China was experiencing turmoil in her bitter Opium War at that time and there seemed no signs of lessening.

It was then that the famous pioneer missionary to Africa, Robert Moffat, came to London and visited the home on Aldersgate Street where Livingstone was residing. A warm friendship sprang up [Livingstone later became Moffat's son-in-law] and the China-chosen missionary-to-be attended all the public services of Moffat wherever and whenever he spoke, in addition to asking myriads of questions.

Here is the outcome, as described by Moffat himself: "I had occasion to call for some one at Mrs. Sewell's, a boardinghouse for young missionaries in Aldersgate Street, where Livingstone lived. I observed soon that this young man was interested in my story, that he would sometimes come quietly and ask me a question or two, and then he was always desirous to know where I was to speak in public, and attended on these occasions. By and by he asked me whether I thought he would do for Africa. I said I believed he would, if he would not go to an old station, but would advance to unoccupied ground, specifying the vast plain to the north, where I had sometimes seen, in the morning sun, the smoke of a thousand villages, where no missionary had ever been. At last Livingstone said: 'What is the use of my waiting for the end of this abominable opium war? I will go at once to Africa.' The directors concurred, and Africa became his sphere."

And thus it was that the steps of this good man were delightfully directed to Africa, where the name Livingstone became legendary and where his heart lies buried today—although the rest of his remains are interred with other heroes in Westminster Abbey.

4. THE POEM:
>The human tide goes rushing down to death;
>Turn thou a moment from the current broad
>And listen: What is this the silence saith,

O Soul? 'Be still, and know that I am God.'
The mighty God! Here shalt thou find thy rest,
O weary one! There is naught else to know,
Naught else to seek,—here thou mayest cease thy quest;
Give thyself up; He leads where thou shouldst go.
—*Celia Thaxter* (1836-1894)

14.

1. THE PROMISE: *"For in thee, O Lord, do I hope: thou wilt hear, O Lord my God. For I said, Hear me, lest otherwise they should rejoice over me: when my foot slippeth, they magnify themselves against me"* (Psalm 38:15,16).

2. THE POINT: The Lord has promised to help His own in times of trial and need. This is especially true if the enemies of God will triumph in ridicule should failure be the portion of the saint.

3. THE PROOF: In the late 1700s there was an outstanding Christian businessman in Berlin, Germany, by the name of Daniel Loest. His integrity was unquestioned and his zeal for serving and pleasing God extended to the abandonment of part of his lucrative business, because it involved partial desecration of the Lord's Day. On one occasion he faced a very crucial financial dilemma and here is the fascinating account, in his own words, of how he met it:

"One day the Baron von Kottwitz, a friend of mine, entered my establishment, and requested me to give security for a certain wealthy Christian lady, who was in a financial strait. He said that her attorney would give me all the necessary information as to her financial standing, etc., and that nothing more was required than my signature to the note of six hundred dollars. I did not have much faith in the attorney. However, as I desired to lend a helping hand to Christian friends in need, I went to his office. I found him reading the Scripture, which was very surprising to me. He asserted that he was well acquainted with the lady, that she owned much real estate, and there was not the least danger for me to become her security. In good faith I now set my name to a note for six hundred dollars.

"Several months had elapsed, when one day I received an order from the court to pay the note of six hundred dollars on the following Tuesday. I now discovered that the lady was largely indebted, and I had been selected as the victim of a common fraud. It was particularly hard to furnish the money at so short notice, since I had already accepted a draft of three hundred dollars due on the following Saturday.

"I hastened to the home of a friend, whom I already owed five hundred, to ask him for a further loan. On my way there I met a friend, whom I owed four hundred dollars, and he requested me to return the loan by Friday, so that he could meet a certain payment.

" 'You shall have it,' I sighed, and hastened on.

"When I reached the home of my friend, he came toward me with these words: 'Mr. Loest, I am glad you have come; I was just coming to see you. I wish you could return me the loan of the five hundred dollars on Wednesday. I desire to pay up a mortgage on my house.'

"Without telling him what had brought me hither, I promised him the money, and left. I scarcely knew what to do. It now occurred to me that a wholesale merchant, an intimate friend of mine, had recently died. As it happened, I was indebted to this house also for goods received; a note of five hundred dollars was about due; and besides there was an open account of about three hundred dollars. However, I expected that his widow could give me relief in this hour of need, so I went to her.

"When I arrived there, she handed me an order from the court, demanding the payment of the five-hundred-dollar note on the following Thursday. Then she added: 'Mr. Loest, I desire very much the payment of the open account also, at least by Saturday morning, as there are at present so many payments for me to make, besides the costs of the funeral,' etc.

" 'I shall attend to all,' I replied, and also left her house.

"The reader may wonder how I could carry the burden that was continually growing greater and heavier upon me, without sinking into despair. I saw in it the divine providence, and believed firmly that the Heavenly Father would deliver me to the honor and glory of His holy name. I had gone out to borrow six hundred dollars, and, when I returned, my payments for the ensuing week stood thus: six hundred dollars on Tuesday; five hundred dollars on Wednesday; five hundred dollars on Thursday; four hundred dollars on Friday; three hundred dollars on Saturday morning, and three hundred dollars on Saturday afternoon—making a total of two thousand six hundred dollars. This was on Saturday, and the cash drawer contained between three and four dollars.

"Meditating for awhile what to do, my mind was suddenly drawn upon a wealthy broker, whom I knew as one willing to lend money at a reasonable rate of interest. I went to him, expecting to borrow two thousand dollars. I knew him to be a scoffer and an enemy of the Christian faith; still it seemed I was compelled to go to him for this loan.

"I had scarcely made my request when he very sarcastically replied: 'What, you, Mr. Loest, in financial difficulties? or any difficulties whatever? I cannot believe that. It is simply impossible. You have upon all occasions boasted of your rich Heavenly Father; why don't you go to Him now in the hour of need; He will surely help you!'

" 'You are right,' I said, 'I beg your pardon for disturbing your peace.'

"With this I hastened home, and, entering my closet, I earnestly sought for pardon from my Heavenly Father for seeking human help rather than first bringing my case to Him in prayer. I then earnestly sought deliverance in this hour of need. My faith was strengthened and I firmly believed that deliverance would come.

"And it did come. Early on Monday morning I noticed that my helpers had all they could do in the store and I hastened to their assistance. Thus it continued all day. When late in the evening the last customer had left and the money was counted, I found the cash sales for the day amounted to six hundred and three dollars and fourteen groschen. Thus the six hundred dollars for payment due on Tuesday morning were ready and I could not help praising the Lord.

"On Tuesday morning my store was again filled with customers, and we were extremely busy all day. There was no time for regular meals so we each took a lunch by turn. In the evening I had the five hundred dollars necessary for the Wednesday payment, and there were but two dollars left.

"And thus it continued all week. Friends came into my store and bought a full supply, who had never bought of me before. Many old accounts which had long since been considered worthless, were paid during this week. Whenever another bill of this kind was paid, I said to myself, 'It is the Lord; praise His name, O my soul!' And strange it was that the sales of each day amounted to just the amount payable on the following day, never leaving over two or three dollars in the treasury. When the three hundred dollars were paid on Saturday morning, there were just two dollars and twenty groschen left.

"There were still three hundred dollars to be paid that afternoon. But on this day not a customer entered the store. It seemed as though everybody was now supplied and nobody desired to buy. At three o'clock we only had the two dollars in the drawer, and at four o'clock I knew the agent would present the draft for payment. This was another severe trial.

"But, behold, deliverance came. It was a quarter to four when a little old woman entered the store and said to me: 'Mr. Loest, I am living here close by in a little room all by myself. I have had a few dollars paid me, and I wish very much you would take care of the money for me.'

" 'I will cheerfully do so,' I replied; 'I will write you a deposit certificate. How large is the sum?'

" 'Oh, there are only three hundred dollars; I will go and get them.'

"After a few minutes she returned with the money and received her certificate. She was scarcely gone when the agent came and presented the draft, which was immediately paid with this money. I stood lost in admiration and love to my Heavenly Father. I was compelled to call out, 'How wonderful are thy ways, O Lord!' This had, indeed, been a week of wonderful deliverances to me.

"But another wonderful help was yet to come. My stock was now very low, and so was also my treasury. All looked-for payments had been made, and the demand would probably not be very great during the next three months. So what could I do?

"In this hour of need another merchant who desired to leave Berlin offered me his entire stock of goods, payments to be made at my convenience. I accepted this offer, and the trade proved a very profitable one. Prices advancing on some of the goods, I had soon earned back the six hundred dollars of which I had been defrauded and was able to make my payments before they were really due.

"I praise the Lord with all my heart for His wonderful deliverances. 'Praise the Lord, O my soul, and all that is within me, praise his holy name!' "

4. THE POEM:
>He knows when joyful hours are best,
>   He sends them as He sees it meet;
>When thou hast borne the fiery test,
>   And art made free from all deceit,
>He comes to thee all unaware,
>   And makes thee own His loving care.
>
>   —*Georg Neumark* (1621-1681)

15.

1. THE PROMISE: *"Blessed is he that considereth the poor: the Lord will deliver him in time of trouble"* (Psalm 41:1).

2. THE POINT: Our wonderful Lord offers special protection and special help to those who themselves grant help to the needy. It is interesting that the verse preceding this promise contains a reminder of how God has helped us poor and needy sinners, saying, "But I am poor and needy; yet the Lord thinketh upon me: thou art my help and my deliverer. . ." (Psalm 40:17).

3. THE PROOF: Oswald Chambers was born in Scotland nearly a century ago. He was converted in his teens on his way home from hearing the great Charles Spurgeon in London. Educated at the little-known Dunoon Training College, he learned to walk with God and manifested a tremendous life of faith before God called him Home at the early age of 43. The world will forever be indebted to him for his masterful book of devotions, *My Utmost for His Highest,* one of the most popular and widely-circulated devotional volumes ever published.

One of the characteristics of faith he possessed, which made him refer to himself as "a fool for God," pertained to his habit of giving to every one who asked of him. On one occasion, approached by a beggar who gave him a highly illusory story of need, Chambers gave him the very last coin he owned, saying as he did so: "I don't believe your story, but I do believe in obeying God."

When his mother chided him for his seeming folly, the obedient one replied: "God gives me double for all I give away."

What happened?

The very next morning's mail brought a contribution containing more than he had given away! How he rejoiced in the proof of the faithfulness of God to the obedience of His saints.

4. THE POEM:

>**Who does God's work, will get God's pay,**
>**However long may seem the day,**

>   However weary be the way;
> Though powers and Princes thunder 'nay,'
> Who does God's work will get God's pay.
>
> He does not pay as others pay,
>   In gold, or land, or raiment gay,
>   In goods that vanish and decay;
> But God in wisdom knows a way,
> And that is sure, let come what may,
> Who does God's work will get God's pay.
>
> —*Dennis McCarthy*

16.

1. THE PROMISE: *"Come, behold the works of the Lord, what desolations he hath made in the earth. He maketh wars to cease unto the end of the earth; he breaketh the bow, and cutteth the spear in sunder; he burneth the chariot in the fire. Be still, and know that I am God: I will be exalted among the heathen, I will be exalted in the earth"* (Psalm 46:8-10).

2. THE POINT: Jehovah rules and overrules in the battles of earth. He is able to turn the tide in any warfare among nations at any moment. Certain victory can be turned into humiliating defeat, or vice versa, in only minutes. To the victor may belong the spoils, but to God belongs the glory!

3. THE PROOF: In the January, 1944, issue of *The Readers' Digest* appeared a fascinating article entitled, "A Drink That Made History." It was written by Peter W. Rainier, an English engineer in charge of supplying fresh water for the British forces in Africa during World War II. It seems that the British were credited with stopping the German advance through North Africa toward Alexandria at El Alamein; Rainier says it didn't happen that way at all.

The date was July 3, 1942. Rommel and his German troups had battered through the British lines and advanced more than half the 50 miles toward Alexandria where supplies and rest awaited them. Suddenly a remnant of British soldiers confronted the German advance and a battle raged. Although the forces were fairly evenly matched, the balance of fire-power weighed on the side of the Germans.

When it appeared that another five or ten minutes would break the British line, suddenly an incredible incident took place. Approximately 1,100 of Rommel's famed Afrika Korps came stumbling into the British lines with hands held high in the traditional surrender position. Without waiting for capitulation formalities, the captives began ripping canteens from the hips and necks of British soldiers, pouring precious water down swollen throats.

What had caused the strange behavior and surrender?

Prophecy magazine described it: "These men had already been a full day without water when the day before they had broken through the British lines. They found among the British defenses a six-inch water pipe line, much of it above ground for two miles. They shot holes in it and gorged themselves with water. So parched and benumbed were their tongues and throats that they did not detect that the water was salt until the damage had been done.

"After a night of unutterable suffering they were ready to sacrifice any military object for water that would quench their thirst. When they saw their tanks falter and turn back, the infantry could endure the agony no longer, and rushed into the British lines.

"But how did it come to pass that that pipe-line was carrying salt water? Major Rainier is able to tell us, for he built the line. It was new, and undergoing its first test. In that parched country the Major never wasted fresh water in testing out a new line; instead, he used sea water.

"These German soldiers would have found the pipe empty a day later. Who timed the happenings just as they were? Has Fate that much of partiality for the side of right?"

Major Rainier evidently thought so. He closed his article with the words: "On so small a turn of fate is history written."

Christians, on the basis of the above promise, know better. The sentence is true only when the word "God" is substituted for the word "fate."

4. THE POEM:
> Before Thy breath like blazing flux,
> Man and his marvels pass away;
> And changing Empires wane and wax
> Are founded, flourish and decay.
> Redeem thine hours—thy space is brief,
> While in thy glass the sand-grains shiver,
> And measureless thy joy or grief
> When time and thou shalt part for ever.
>
> —*Sir Walter Scott* (1771-1832)

17.

1. THE PROMISE: *"Offer unto God thanksgiving; and pay thy vows unto the most High: And call upon me in the day of trouble: I will deliver thee, and thou shalt glorify me"* (Psalm 50:14,15).

2. THE POINT: The Christian who maintains proper relationship with the Lord—specifically in the areas of praise and practice—need never fear ANY day of trouble. Deliverance in such an hour, when requested, is guaranteed. The delivered one will then, of course, give proper credit to the Deliverer. The context reminds us that He has the resources of the world and its fulness behind Him.

3. THE PROOF: Dr. Robert G. Lee, one of the South's greatest preachers, worked at home on his father's farm until he was twenty-one. Then, with only an eighth grade education, he determined to earn enough money to attend a college preparatory school. He went to Panama for nine months and

made the big wages which work on the canal offered. After nine months he returned with a substantial sum, only to learn that his father was under heavy monetary pressures. Without a second thought he turned over the entire amount to his father, save for enough to pay the school's enrollment fees and buy books. Throughout prep school and college he was forced to work long and strenuous hours—along with his studies—to pay his bills.

Things sometimes got rough! On one occasion, when he had a student pastorate added to his other responsibilities, he received a note from the dean reminding him that $84 on his university bill was "long due and unpaid." He was advised that, since the auditors were going to be at school the following week, "Please see to it that we have the $84.00 you owe by next Monday at noon." While not such an enormous sum for today's collegiates, it was a fantastic amount back in 1910.

Young Lee was beside himself. He later described it as follows:

"When I went to Latin class there seemed to be an 84 on each of the glasses Professor Martin wore—nose glasses that seemed to perch perilously on the bridge of his nose. The professor called on me to put into English some Latin words in paragraph 184, which words were 'puella exima forma,' a girl of exceptional beauty. I was not thinking of any girl, far or near, of exceptional beauty. I was thinking only of the $84.00 I owed. When the Latin class was dismissed, I went to my room—room No. 3—in Griffith cottage. The three above my door looked like an 84. I bolted the door. I looked at the little old alarm clock which had faithfully awakened me at 3 a.m. each day so that I could get ready to carry the newspapers. It was ticking industriously—and it seemed to be saying: 84, 84, 84, 84.

"I pulled down the shades and got down on my knees beside my bed—to ask help of God. I knew nobody in the world to whom I could go and get $84.00. I thanked God for saving me. I talked to Him about calling me to be a preacher—and I was at Furman to try to get an education to help me preach.

"I didn't say any of these little 'Polly-wants-a-cracker'

prayers. I was at my wits end. I was reeling to and fro—and felt so helpless.

"Next morning—Saturday—I took the little Swamp Rabbit train for the mountain railroad station. There I was met by one of the Goodwin family and taken to their two-story mountain home. Now you can't play Beethoven's *Ninth Symphony* on a tin whistle. But this I'll say, Mrs. Sallie Goodwin, whom I called my 'second mother' and whose picture is framed with my own mother's and my wife's mother, is in my library today. She said to me—after supper and prayer—'Mister Lee, I don't know why I had not thought of it before, but yesterday I got to thinking about your working your way through school—and you might need a little money.' I said: 'Yes, Ma'am.' Then, not knowing how desperately were her young pastor's financial circumstances, this godly woman gave the young pastor twenty five-dollar gold pieces—money she had stored up over a period of years.

"Talk about your beautiful sunrises and gorgeous sunsets! The glories of both combined could not equal the beauty of that gold money in my hands. I began to laugh and to cry. And it is none of your business what else I did. But after thanks and good nights were spoken, I went up the stairway to my room. And then on the old-fashioned bed, covered with a quilt in which were many squares of cloth of various colors, I put a five-dollar gold piece in twenty of the squares and knelt down and, after viewing that golden landscape o'er, thanked God for answered prayer—and for such a friend in time of trouble as was this precious widow who did as much for me as ever did the 'widow woman' of Zarephath for Elijah."

He had his $84 for the school, $10 tithe. . .and $6 left over!

4. THE POEM:

    I know that trial works for ends
      Too high for sense to trace,
   That oft in dark attire He sends
      Some embassy of grace;
   May none depart till I have gained
      The blessing which it bears,

> And learn, though late, I entertained
> An angel unawares.
> —*James Drummond Burns* (1823-1864)

[1] ROBERT G. LEE: A CHOSEN VESSEL by E. Schuyler English. Copyright 1949 by Zondervan Publishing House, Grand Rapids, Michigan. Used by permission.

18.

1. THE PROMISE: *"Thou hast been a shelter for me, and a strong tower from the enemy. I will abide in thy tabernacle for ever: I will trust in the covert of thy wings. Selah"* (Psalm 61:3,4).

2. THE POINT: God has special protection for His own. As Satan complained to God about Job, the Lord has placed a protective hedge about the redeemed and nothing can happen to them apart from the permissive will of God. Again and again, sometimes in matters known and undoubtedly much more frequently completely unknown to the individual, God's wondrous hand of protection rules and overrules.

3. THE PROOF: Nicholas Smith, in his book, *Hymns Historically Famous*, recounts this true experience: The *Boston Globe* published a story of more than unusual interest showing the influence of "Jesus, Lover of My Soul." A few years ago a number of Civil War veterans were passengers on a Mississippi steamer (not on an Atlantic steamer as commonly stated), when one evening the company, discussing the question whether there was such a thing as a special Providence, an old soldier related this incident:

"During the Atlanta campaign in 1864, I was called on one night for sentinel duty. It was frightfully dark, the enemy was near, the country full of pitfalls, and I knew that my life was in momentary peril. Of course, I had faced just as great risks many times before, but somehow on this particular night I began to dwell upon the danger that surrounded me, until I was in a state of nervous collapse. In an effort to calm my fears I began to sing 'Jesus, Lover of My Soul,' very much on the principle of a boy who whistles in going through the woods. I sang the hymn through to the end, and by the time I had finished it, I was perfectly calm and fearless."

Among the listeners to this story was an ex-Confederate soldier who, at the close, asked: "Did you say that happened before Atlanta in 1864?"

"Yes."

"Well, my friend, I was in the Confederate army stationed at Atlanta. I was reconnoitering one night when I chanced to pass near a sentinel of the Northern army at his post. I had determined to pop him over, and was bringing my gun to my shoulder, when I heard him sing the words,

Cover my defenseless head
With the shadow of Thy wing.

I quickly dropped my gun, saying to myself: 'I can't kill that man were he ten times my enemy.' "

It was a pathetic scene when the ex-Confederate finished his story, and the two old veterans of opposing armies instinctively clasped each other by the hand. Tears of gratitude came to the eyes of the Union soldier when he heard how his hymn-prayer had saved his life.

4. THE POEM:

>Jesus, Lover of my Soul,
> Let me to Thy bosom fly,
>While the nearer waters roll,
> While the tempest still is high!
>Hide me, O my Savior, hide,
> Till the storm of life be past;
>Safe into the haven guide,
> O receive my soul at last!
>
>Other refuge have I none,
> Hangs my helpless soul on Thee:
>Leave, ah! leave me not alone,
> Still support and comfort me!

> All my trust on Thee is stayed,
>   All my help from Thee I bring:
> Cover my defenseless head
>   With the shadow of Thy wing.
>
> Wilt Thou not regard my call?
>   Wilt Thou not accept my prayer?
> Lo! I sink, I faint, I fall—
>   Lo! on Thee I cast my care:
> Reach me out Thy gracious hand!
>   While I of Thy strength receive,
> Hoping against hope I stand,
>   Dying, and, behold, I live!
>   —*Charles Wesley* (1707-1788)

19.

1. THE PROMISE: *"Surely the wrath of man shall praise thee: the remainder of wrath shalt thou restrain"* (Psalm 76:10).

2. THE POINT: God is not only sovereign, He is all powerful. He can take the spewings of hatred from puny mortals—Ebenezer Erskine points out that the original has it "the wrath of clay," weak, impotent man—and turn those assaults by a blasphemer, an infidel or an atheist into the very workings which result in praise and glory to Him. And He can cut short a feeble mortal's wrath whenever He pleases.

3. THE PROOF: Sometimes truth is stranger than fiction! Such was the case in the conversion of Adoniram Judson. Born of Congregational ministerial parents, a brilliant intellect, graduating as valedictorian from Providence College (now Brown University) while still in his teens, his exaggerated ego made him a likely candidate for the wave of French infidelity sweeping American campuses at the start of the nineteenth century.

At Providence he fell in with a young man by the name of Ernest, equally gifted and brilliant, and it was not long until

Judson had abandoned the "faith of his fathers" to become an outspoken champion of atheism. Graduating a year after his friend, he decided to tour several states on horseback before settling down in a life vocation. For a period of weeks he traveled with a troup of strolling players, then struck out on his own.

Stopping for lodging one night at a country inn, the host explained that his only vacant room was right next to a very seriously ill gentleman who might not make it through the night.

"That's all right. I'm an atheist," boasted Judson. "Death has no terrors for me."

However, the youth who thought he had dismissed God from his life received much more than he bargained for that night. The paper-thin partition brought the dying man's agonizing groans of terror, hopelessness and despair into his room as clearly as if he had been in a bed beside him.

His first thought was that he should try to aid him. But how? What could he say? His theology of atheism would be no comfort to such an one at such an hour. In fact, he felt a twinge of embarrassment for even considering such a thing. How his witty, brilliant friend, Ernest, would chide him if he heard about it!

So he pulled the covers over his head to silence the awful cries, but to no avail. The moans, the shrieks, the agonizing wails pierced the ears of the sleepless Judson until about dawn, when suddenly they stopped. Not much later he dressed and went to inquire from the landlord as to the fate of his neighbor for the night.

"He's dead," the innkeeper said.

"Dead?" whispered the startled self-styled atheist. "Do you know who he was?"

"Yes, he was a young man by the name of Ernest, a graduate of Providence College."

Shocked, stunned by the revelation, he rode through the countryside with the words ringing in his heart and soul, "Dead, *dead!* Lost, *lost!* Ernest is *dead.* Ernest is *lost* forever!" If any man ever preached himself under conviction, Judson did. The result was that he returned home to his godly father and mother, begging them to explain how he might obtain peace with God. Next, he went to Andover Seminary, then he and his bride of 7 days set sail with Luther Rice, James Richards, Gordon Hall and Samuel Mills for Calcutta to labor for Christ as America's first foreign missionaries. Judson eventually found his place of service in Burma, accomplishing one of the greatest missionary ministries of all time.

4. THE POEM:

> I had walked life's way with an easy tread,
> Had followed where comforts and pleasures led,
> Until one day in a quiet place
> I met the Master face to face.
>
> With station and rank and wealth for my goal,
> Much thought for my body but none for my soul,
> I had entered to win in life's mad race,
> When I met the Master face to face.
>
> I met Him and knew Him and blushed to see
> That His eyes full of sorrow were fixed on me,
> And I faltered and fell at His feet that day
> While my castles melted and vanished away.
>
> Melted and vanished, and in their place,
> Naught else did I see but the Master's face;
> And I cried aloud, "Oh, make me meet
> To follow the steps of Thy wounded feet."
>
> My thought is now for the souls of men;
> I have lost my life to find it again,
> E'er since one day in a quiet place
> I met the Master face to face.

20.

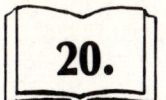

1. THE PROMISE: *"Blessed is the man whose strength is in thee; in whose heart are the ways of them. Who passing through the valley of Baca make it a well; the rain also filleth the pools. They go from strength to strength, every one of them in Zion appeareth before God"* (Psalm 84:5-7).

2. THE POINT: There never has been—and there never will be—a situation confronting a child of God too difficult to be met by the available strength of Jehovah. No "Valley of Tears" need be a "mission impossible" when such plentiful grace is freely available. Nor are His sources of supply ever limited!

3. THE PROOF: It was during the early days of World War II. Japan had invaded China and her advancing troops wrought untold terror in the hearts of the cities' inhabitants lying in their paths. In one such city a group of missionaries joined the natives in hurried evacuation, some walking and some on bicycles—but all heavily laden with bundles and suitcases. The senior missionary sought to buy passage for them on one of the many trucks lumbering along the crowded road, but his money could not obtain it. "No more room—no more room," the drivers shouted as they sped past.

One white-headed missionary, who had risen from a sickbed to flee, managed to get several miles out of the city when a steep hill loomed before her. Desperately weak, she realized not only that she could not make it, but that when night fell and the others became aware she was missing, they would wait and she would hold them up. Not only so, but the Japanese were close behind.

Suddenly she remembered a passage from an Oswald Chambers book: "Lord, show Thyself sufficient for this crisis now." Immediately she applied the thought to her own needs, giving special emphases, "Lord, show Thyself sufficient for this crisis now." At that moment a truck appeared from around a bend in the road. Like all the other trucks it was so overloaded there seemed no possible space for another human.

However, a tall, gracious Chinese gentleman slid off the truck and said to the missionary, "We are going slowly enough for you to get on. Let me help you." In a moment she was safely aboard the lumbering truck.

"I have a white-haired missionary friend who is also walking up ahead," the grateful lady announced. "We will pick her up, too," the new friend replied. And he did!

Later, when the truck overtook the other missionaries in the party, struggling along on their bicycles with their heavy loads, the missionary called, "Throw up the suitcases—throw them up here!" The senior missionary sized up the situation in a moment and hurriedly obeyed the order, making the load of the others so much easier.

As the missionary rode on, cheerfully waving as the truck passed her companions, she joyfully thought: "How wonderful! I thought I would hold them up and now, instead, I am 'helping' them!" Later she learned that her benefactor, a Chinese official, had once been befriended by white people and he had never forgotten the kindness. God had seen to it that the one Chinese in all the area who could and would help in those circumstances was present at the exact moment of need.

4. THE POEM:

Lord, is it still the right way, though I cannot see Thy face,
Though I do not feel Thy presence and Thine all-sustaining grace?
Can even this be leading through the bleak and sunless wild
To the City of Thy holy rest, the mansions undefiled?

I cannot hear Thy voice, Lord! dost Thou still hear my cry?
I cling to Thine assurance that Thou art ever nigh;
I know that Thou art faithful; I trust but cannot see
That it is still the right way by which Thou leadest me.

—Frances Ridley Havergal (1836-1879)

21. 1. THE PROMISE: *"For the Lord God is a sun and shield: the Lord will give grace and glory: no good thing will he withhold from them that walk uprightly"* (Psalm 84:11).

2. THE POINT: Jehovah God is all the believer needs since he has everything in Him. He provides grace for the present and He has promised glory for the future. Because of this, the child of God who obediently and faithfully walks in paths of righteousness can be assured of the answer regarding any and every good thing for which he prays.

3. THE PROOF: D. L. Moody told of a man in Scotland who was fired repeatedly from his jobs because of drink. Finally, mistakenly thinking that if he changed his environment it would solve his problem, he left his wife and two daughters and sailed for America with his seven-year-old son, Johnnie. One of his first acts after arriving in this country was to seek out a saloon and get drunk. In that condition, he got separated from the boy and was never heard from again.

The authorities sent the lad to an institution and later he was farmed out as an apprentice in Massachusetts. Eventually he ran off to sea and later went to Chicago to work on the lakes. Someone invited him to a gospel service and he was soundly converted to Christ.

When he got right with God, he became anxious to find his mother. One day, after writing fruitlessly to a number of places in Scotland, he found this promise in Psalm 84:11. Closing his Bible, he fell to his knees and cried: "O God, I have been trying to walk uprightly for months past; help me to find my mother." Suddenly the thought struck him: write back to the place in Massachusetts where you used to live! He did and they sent him a letter from Scotland that had arrived seven years before. He wrote to that address and a letter from his sister arrived by return mail.

Moody described it:

"I would like you to have seen him when he got that letter. He brought it to me; and the tears flowed so that he could scarcely read it. His sister had written on behalf of the mother; she had been so overcome by the tidings of her long lost boy that she could not write.

"The sister said that all the nineteen years he had been away, his mother had prayed to God day and night that he might be saved, and that she might live to know what had become of him, and see him once more. Now, said the sister, she was so overjoyed, not only that he was alive, but that he had become a Christian. It was not long before the mother and sisters came out to Chicago to meet him.

"I mention this incident to show how God answers prayer. This mother cried to God for nineteen long years. It must have seemed to her sometimes as though God did not mean to give her the desire of her heart; but she kept praying, and at last the answer came."

4. THE POEM:

> He who hath led will lead
> All through the wilderness;
> He who hath fed will feed;
> He who hath blessed will bless;
> He who hath heard thy cry
> Will never close His ear;
> He who hath marked thy faintest sigh
> Will not forget thy tear.
> He loveth always, faileth never,
> So rest on Him today, forever.
> —*Frances Ridley Havergal* (1836-1879)

22. 1. THE PROMISE: *"Give ear, O Lord, unto my prayer; and attend to the voice of my supplications. In the day of my trouble I will call upon thee: for thou wilt answer me"* (Psalm 86:6,7).

2. THE POINT: All God's children experience repeatedly what the psalmist called "the day of my trouble." Again and again we find ourselves faced with circumstances way beyond and above us. In such times we can call upon the Lord with the firm assurance "thou WILT answer."

3. THE PROOF: Our youngest son, Ron, was accepted by the Association of Baptists for World Evangelism to participate in its missionary apprenticeship program the summer between his junior and senior years in college in Peru, South America. He began getting his shots, had passport pictures taken, etc., and got ready to make his application for a passport.

His birth certificate was nowhere to be found!

Mrs. Sumner wrote the Department of Vital Statistics in Austin, Texas, enclosing a check to cover the cost of a duplicate copy. Two or three weeks went by and back came a letter, enclosing our check. It seemed that the fee had gone up and the check was 50¢ or so short. We were advised to reorder, sending the correct fee. Mrs. Sumner did so, giving instructions for the certificate to be sent to our son at school, since the college was helping with many of the details.

When school dismissed in June, it still hadn't arrived. Since Ron was to leave at the end of the month for South America and the situation was becoming more acute by the hour, we determined to search for the original, which Ron had used three years before in obtaining a job at a factory. All the drawers at home were ransacked, along with boxes in the attic. The safe at our office, where some of our important papers are kept, was minutely searched.

No birth certificate!

We called the college and no mail had been forwarded from there, meaning the duplicate's arrival was at least three days away, at very best. We decided to make prayer for the original a very definite thing. That night, in the men's prayer group at our church, intercession was earnestly made in behalf of the certificate. Additional prayer was requested and offered during the main prayer service.

The very next morning, when we arrived at the office, we were impressed to search the secretary's desk. Starting with the bottom drawer first, we were only about halfway through when the missing birth certificate was in hand. The passport application was made the same day at the federal building in Indianapolis and Ron spent the period ministering, thanks to a God who answers the "trouble call" of His saints, in Peru.

4. THE POEM:

>Be not afraid to pray—to pray is right.
>Pray, if thou canst, with hope; but ever pray,
>Though hope be weak, or sick with long delay;
>Pray in the darkness, if there be no light.
>Far is the time, remote from human sight,
>When war and discord on the earth shall cease;
>Yet every prayer for universal peace
>Avails the blessed time to expedite.
>Whate'er is good to wish, ask that of Heaven,
>Though it be what thou canst not hope to see;
>Pray to be perfect, though material leaven
>Forbid the spirit so on earth to be;
>But if for any wish thou darest not pray,
>Then pray to God to cast that wish away.

—*David Hartley Coleridge* (1796-1849)

23.

1. THE PROMISE: *"Surely he shall deliver thee. . ."* (Psalm 91:3). *"Thou shalt not be afraid. . ."* (Psalm 91:5).

2. THE POINT: The promise of protection and preservation is one thing; the promise of peace and tranquility in the hour of terror is quite another. God promises BOTH to all who dwell in the secret place of the Most High and abide under

His shadow! Deliverence and delight are the portion of the dedicated.

3. THE PROOF: John Gibson Paton was Scotland's missionary gift to the New Hebrides. Born at Kirkmahoe on May 24, 1824—the first of eleven children, three of whom became ministers and all of whom lived godly, useful lives—he first set foot on the soil of his adopted land on August 30, 1858. As a foretaste, perhaps, of things to come, he narrowly missed landing on "an island inhabited by cannibals of a particularly ferocious type, who would certainly have killed and eaten the whole party if they could have laid hands on them."

The people among whom he began his ministry were "savages of the most primitive kind, unclothed, given over to cannibalism and all sorts of unnameable vices, without even the rudiments of a literature, and with no religion except the worship of ancestors and a childish fear of evil spirits whom they tried to propitiate by fetishism of the most debased kind." Women, regarded only as slaves and burden-bearers, were treated with the fiercest cruelty, beaten and abused at the whim of the male, sometimes dying as a result. Widows were commonly put to death. The birth of a baby girl was considered a calamity and frequently infanticide resulted when one was born. The elderly were often put to death openly just to get them out of the way.

Again and again attempts were made on Paton's life. [He finally died a natural death, incidentally, at the ripe old age of eighty-two!] One of his biographers wrote: "It is a literal fact that not for a single hour was his life safe. On one occasion a chief followed him about for four hours with a loaded musket; another day a man suddenly, and for no apparent reason, rushed at him with an axe, and was only prevented from striking him by another native who gallantly defended him from a blow which would probably have meant instant death; and another time he was roused in the night by a chief and his men who were trying to force their way into his house to kill him. They were kept at bay by a retriever dog that had often protected him.

". . .one day, as the missionary was at work near his house, a party of armed men surrounded him, and, at a given signal, every man's musket was levelled at his head. With a courage that could only have been inspired with a consciousness of the presence of God, Mr. Paton calmly went on with his work as though no one was near. The muskets were lowered, and the would-be murderers retired to a little distance, where they seemed to be discussing amongst themselves as to who should fire that first shot; but nothing happened, and after a while the whole party disappeared."

On another occasion, two warring parties (one of whom had been feigning friendliness) united to attack the mission premises, pillaging and destroying almost everything of value Paton possessed. The following day they returned in even greater numbers, thirsting for the missionary's blood. Homeless, destitute and sought by savages who wanted to slay him, Paton spent the night hidden among the branches of a huge chestnut tree. Yet, describing his experience as the natives shouted and fired their guns all around him, Paton said: "I sat there among the branches, as safe in the arms of Jesus. Never, in all my sorrows, did my Lord draw nearer to me, and speak more soothingly in my soul than when the moonlight flickered amongst those chestnut leaves, and the night air played on my throbbing brow, as I told all my heart to Jesus. If it be to glorify my God I will not grudge to spend my nights alone in such a tree, to feel again my Savior's spiritual presence, to enjoy His consoling fellowship."

Perhaps the testimony of the amazed savages, on the occasion of another miraculous deliverance, best sums up the story: "Your Jehovah God alone thus protects you and brings you safely home."

4. THE POEM:

Abide with me! fast falls the eventide;
The darkness thickens; Lord, with me abide!
When other helpers fail, and comforts flee,
Help of the helpless, O abide with me!

Swift to its close ebbs out life's little day;
Earth's joys grow dim, its glories pass away;
Change and decay in all around I see;

O Thou, who changest not, abide with me!

Not a brief glance I beg, a passing word,
But as Thou dwelt with Thy disciples, Lord,
Familiar, condescending, patient, free,
Come not to sojourn but abide with me.

Come not in terrors, as the King of kings;
But kind and good, with healing in Thy wings;
Tears for all woes, a heart for every plea;
Come, Friend of sinners, and abide with me.

Thou on my head in early youth didst smile;
And, though rebellious and perverse meanwhile,
Thou hast not left me, oft as I left Thee;
On to the close, O Lord, abide with me!

I need Thy presence every passing hour;
What but Thy grace can foil the tempter's power?
Who like Thyself my guide and stay can be?
Through cloud and sunshine, O abide with me!

I fear no foe, with Thee at hand to bless,
Ills have no weight, and tears no bitterness;
Where is death's sting? where, grave, thy victory?
I triumph still, if Thou abide with me!

Hold then Thy cross before my closing eyes!
Shine through the gloom, and point me to the skies!
Heaven's morning breaks, and earth's vain shadows flee;
In life, in death, O Lord, abide with me!

—*Henry F. Lyte* (1793-1847)

24. 1. THE PROMISE: *"Blessed is the man that feareth the Lord, that delighteth greatly in his commandments. His seed shall be mighty upon earth: the generation of the upright shall be blessed. Wealth and riches shall be in his house: and his righteousness endureth for ever"* (Psalm 112:1-3).

2. THE POINT: Partnership with God is advantageous in

EVERY avenue of life and some form of prosperity ALWAYS follows such a union of interest. The businessman who fears Jehovah with a godly trust and is obedient to the commands of His Word may rightly expect material prosperity.

3. THE PROOF: Boston's mighty Baptist giant of yesteryear, Dr. Adoniram Judson Gordon, wrote the following: "There is a Christian league in this country, banded together to promote systematic giving. It brings every member into covenant to keep a strict account with the Lord, and to render Him one-tenth of the income. An annual report is made by each member, giving a statement of his business and spiritual prosperity. The secretary recently told us that the results have been surprising even to the most sanguine advocates of the tithing system; that not only has the income of the missionary societies receiving the funds been greatly increased, but that, out of the six thousand entering into this league, all but two or three have reported greatly increased business prosperity.

"We give an instance from a well-known life. Many years ago a lad of sixteen years left home to seek his fortune. As he trudged along, he met an old neighbor, the captain of a canal boat, and the following conversation took place, which changed the whole current of the boy's life:

" 'Well, William, where are you going?'

" 'I don't know,' he answered; 'father is too poor to keep me at home any longer, and says I must now make a living for myself.'

" 'There's no trouble about that,' said the captain. 'Be sure you start right, and you'll get along finely.'

"William told his friend that the only trade he knew anything about was soap and candle making, at which he had helped his father while at home.

" 'Well,' said the old man, 'let me pray with you once more, and give you a little advice, and then I will let you go.'

"They both kneeled down upon the tow path; the dear old man prayed earnestly for William, and then gave this advice: 'Some one will soon be the leading soap maker in New York. It can be you as well as any one. I hope it may. Be a good man; give your heart to Christ; give the Lord all that belongs to Him of every dollar you earn; make an honest soap; give a full pound, and I am certain you will yet be a prosperous and rich man.'

"When the boy arrived in the city, he found it hard to get work. Lonesome and far from home, he remembered his mother's words and the last words of the canal boat captain. He was then led to 'seek first the kingdom of God and His righteousness,' and united with the church. He remembered his promise to the old captain, and the first dollar he earned brought up the question of the Lord's part. In the Bible he found that the Jews were commanded to give one tenth; so he said, 'If the Lord will take one tenth, I will give that.' And so he did; and ten cents of every dollar were sacred to the Lord.

"Having regular employment, he soon became a partner, and after a few years his partners died and William became the sole owner of the business. He now resolved to keep his promise to the old captain; he made an honest soap, gave a full pound, and instructed his bookkeeper to open an account with the Lord, and carry one-tenth of all his income to that account.

"He prospered; his business grew; his family was blessed; his soap sold and he grew rich faster than he had ever hoped. He then gave the Lord two-tenths, and prospered more than ever; then he gave three-tenths, then four-tenths, then five-tenths. He educated his family, settled all his plans for life, and gave all his income to the Lord. He prospered more than ever. This is the story of Mr. William Colgate, who has given millions of dollars to the Lord's cause, and left a name that will never die."

4. THE POEM:
>Give! as the morning that flows out of heaven;
>Give! as the waves when their channel is riven;
>Give! as the free air and sunshine is given;
>>Lavishly, utterly, joyfully give—
>Not the waste drops of thy cup overflowing,
>Not the faint sparks of thy hearth ever glowing,

> Not a pale bud from the June roses blowing—
> Give as He gave thee, who gave thee to live!
> —*Rose Terry Cooke* (1827-1892)

25. 1. THE PROMISE: *"Hear my voice according unto thy lovingkindness: O Lord, quicken* [lit., revive] *me according to thy judgment* [lit., ordinances]" (Psalm 119:149).

2. THE POINT: This verse contains three necessary elements for revival: (1) God's grace: "Thy lovingkindness"; (2) God's Word: "Thy ordinances"; (3) Intercession: "Hear my voice." Note that the human element hinges on intercessory prayer.

3. THE PROOF: Probably one of the most dramatic and best-known illustrations of this truth is the one told by William R. Moody in his biography of his illustrious father, the noted 19th century evangelist, Dwight Lyman Moody. Although the lady in question remains unnamed in the biography, she was a bedfast invalid in perpetual pain, identified elsewhere by Dr. G. Campbell Morgan as Marianne Adlard.

In June of 1872, Moody sailed the second time for England, not intending to minister at all in that country but to see if he could learn more of the Word of God from some of the noted Bible scholars of that land. However, at the close of a prayer meeting at Old Bailey, the pastor of a church in the north of London, a Rev. Lessey, asked Moody if he would minister in his pulpit the following Sunday. Moody consented.

Will Moody, the son, describes the day:

"The morning service seemed very dead and cold. The people did not show much interest, and he felt that it had been a morning lost. But at the next service, which was at half-past six in the evening, it seemed, while he was preaching, as if the very atmosphere was charged with the Spirit of God. There came a hush upon all the people, and a quick response to his words, though he had not been much in prayer that day, and could not understand it.

"When he had finished preaching he asked all who would like to become Christians to rise, that he might pray for them. People rose all over the house until it seemed as if the whole audience was getting up.

"Mr. Moody said to himself: 'These people don't understand me. They don't know what I mean when I ask them to rise.' He had never seen such results before, and did not know what to make of it, so he put the test again.

" 'Now,' he said, 'all of you who want to become Christians just step into the inquiry room.'

"They went in, and crowded the room so that they had to take in extra chairs to seat them all. The minister was surprised, and so was Mr. Moody. Neither had expected such a blessing. They had not realized that God can save by hundreds and thousands as well as by ones and twos.

"When Mr. Moody again asked those that really wanted to become Christians to rise, the whole audience got up. He did not even then know what to do, so he told all who were really in earnest to meet the pastor there the next night.

"The next day he went over to Dublin, but on Tuesday morning received a dispatch urging him to return, saying there were more inquirers on Monday than on Sunday. He went back and held meetings for ten days, and four hundred were taken into that church."

When all the facts were in, it was learned that the bedridden Miss Adlard had been praying for revival in her church for some time. One day she read an account in *Revival* (later called *The Christian*) of the work Moody was doing in Chicago among ragged children. Although she had never heard of Moody before and had no possible way of communicating with him directly, she placed that paper under her pillow and began storming Heaven's

Gate with the entreaty, "O Lord, send this man to our Church!"

On the Sunday of Moody's sermon, when Marianne's sister returned from the morning service, the bedfast saint inquired about the service and her sister replied, "Who do you think preached this morning?" Suggesting several men who had filled the pulpit before, and receiving a negative response, the sister finally revealed, "It was Mr. Moody, from America."

On learning this, Miss Adlard spent the entire afternoon in fervent intercession. This explained the difference between the dead morning service and the Holy Spirit empowered evening one.

Dr. G. Campbell Morgan, who was later her pastor at New Court, tells of visiting her before a trip to America in 1901. She asked him to hand her the "birthday book" and he turned to February 5 and saw the familiar scrawl of the evangelist, "D. L. Moody, Psalm 91." She said, "He wrote that for me when he came to see me in 1872, and I prayed for him every day till he went Home to God." Then she asked Morgan to sign on the date of his birth, covenanting to do the same for him.

4. THE POEM:

>Saints are like roses when they flush rarest,
>Saints are like lilies when they bloom fairest,
>Saints are like violets sweetest of their kind.
> Bear in mind
> This today. Then tomorrow—
>All like roses rarer than the rarest,
>All like lilies fairer than the fairest,
>All like violets sweeter than we know.
> Be it so.
> Tomorrow blots out sorrow.
>
>   —*Christina Georgina Rossetti* (1830-1894)

26. 1. THE PROMISE: *"The Lord shall preserve thee from all evil: he shall preserve thy soul. The Lord shall preserve thy going out and thy coming in from this time forth, and even for evermore"* (Psalm 121:7,8).

2. THE POINT: Preservation is included in the Christian's birthright. While this most certainly does not mean evil will never come into a believer's life, it does mean he will eventually emerge victorious. Satan cannot harm in any way, as the Book of Job so beautifully reveals, one of God's own apart from God's all-wise permission. And, fortunately, preservation from "all evil" includes the wicked vileness emitting from devilish tongues.

3. THE PROOF: One of Satan's most effective tools in silencing one who is doing a real job for God has been, over the years, false slander. The worldling has always been eager to believe the worst about one of God's servants, no matter how absurd the story might be. Often the damage is seemingly irreparable, no matter how innocent the victim.

In the exciting biography of "Uncle John" Vassar, the following is related:

"He went to one place which had long been under the blight of spiritual declension, and where among the youth of the community there was not a single professing Christian. He was informed that the leading spirit in the social life of the place was a young woman—that her influence was commanding, and that it was used against religion. If she could be won to Christ, a great point would be gained.

"So Uncle John went to see her first. As soon as she understood the object of his visit, she rudely refused to listen to him, and bade him begone forthwith without another word. He left her, and went calling elsewhere.

"And presently about everybody he met treated him coldly. At a number of houses he was denied admission, in one instance with violent words. He did not know what to make of it. But the explanation soon came out. The young woman he had first visited, in her extreme anger at him, had declared that he had offered her an insult, and the falsehood was going the rounds, and was everywhere ahead of him.

"This fact, he said when he first discovered it, seemed to him the most mysterious providence he had ever heard of. 'O Lord, what does it mean?' he cried in dismay. His work was completely blocked. There was no help for it; and he had to go.

"Wondering greatly, but submitting, he went to another field some distance away, and began laboring there. He had been there awhile, and was seeing hopeful signs of good, when one evening as he was holding a meeting in a schoolhouse, he heard a large, heavily-loaded sleigh drive up and stop at the door.

"When the door was opened, there appeared a party of some twenty young people, with the young woman before mentioned at their head. Mr. Vassar's first thought was that they had come to mob him or do him harm of some sort.

"They came in, the whole company, all strangers, and the silence that followed was broken by the young woman standing forth and saying, in a trembling voice, 'Mr. Vassar, I have brought these friends of mine with me to hear me ask your forgiveness for the great wrong I did you when you were in our place. Telling that lie was the meanest thing I ever did. That I could tell it, and that I felt like telling it, for such a cause, showed me as I never saw it before, the wickedness of my heart—my state as a sinner. It has led me, I trust, to ask God's forgiveness, and I hope that for Christ's sake He has heard my prayer. Will you forgive me, too?' "[1]

Uncle John was vindicated. His reputation was restored in the community where it had been unjustly tarnished. A young woman was led to see her total sinfulness and was brought to Christ. And an opening was made in an area—*especially among the youth*—where the door had seemed hopelessly closed to the Gospel. What evidence of God's "preserving" power!

4. THE POEM:
O thou of little faith, God has not failed thee yet;

When all looks dark and gloomy, thou dost soon forget—
Forget that He has led thee, and gently cleared thy way;
On clouds has poured His sunshine, and turned thy night to day.
And if He's helped thee hitherto, He will not fail thee now;
How it must wound His loving heart to see thy anxious brow!
O doubt not any longer, to Him commit thy way,
Whom in the past thou trusted, and is "the same. . .today."

[1] From UNCLE JOHN VASSAR OR THE FIGHT OF FAITH by Thomas E. Vassar. Copyright, 1931. Reprinted by permission of the American Tract Society, Oradell, New Jersey.

27. 1. THE PROMISE: *"Cause me to hear thy lovingkindness in the morning; for in thee do I trust: cause me to know the way wherein I should walk; for I lift up my soul unto thee"* (Psalm 143:8).

2. THE POINT: Some things regarding the believer's walk are clearly and definitely stated in the Word of God. There need be no doubt about them because His will in those areas is a matter of revelation. On the other hand, there are many areas of life where the Christian cannot turn to a passage of Scripture and find the will of the Lord. In those instances, because of the saint's sureness of the Father's loving interest, he can lift his soul to God and receive direction as to "the way wherein I should walk."

3. THE PROOF: Stanley Tam owns and operates the States Smelting and Refining Corporation, United States Plastic, and the WTGN radio station in Lima, Ohio. He is a millionaire!

That was not always true!

In fact, when he first started salvaging silver from photographic negatives—with a sideline of collecting outdated studio negatives and re-selling them to a firm that converted them into billfold identification covers—he had the same financial problems which are common to America's under-privileged today.

On one occasion he pulled into Valparaiso, Indiana, with about $80 worth of old negatives. He took them to the warehouse of the firm salvaging them, got a slip with the proper information recorded, then went to the company office for his money. However, the officer authorized to sign the checks was out of town and the receptionist said she would have to mail him the money later.

Tam had exactly 13¢ in his pocket and approximately two gallons of gas in his automobile! Lima was more than 175 miles away and even today's mini-cars don't get 88 miles to a gallon!

What should he do? This was one of the situations where it is not possible to open the Bible and find the answer. So Tam "lifted up his soul" to God for guidance.

Impressed immediately that he should start for Lima, he pulled out of the parking lot and headed for the outskirts of Valparaiso. But the flickering gas gauge, so precariously near the fatal "E," drove him off the road for a second season of prayer. The strong impression from God during that session of intercession remained the same: head for home.

There was a small restaurant across the street and he decided to get one of that day's nickel hamburgers, washed down with a glass of water, before leaving town. Next, he pulled into a gas station and asked if they would sell him eight cents worth of gas, since that was all the money he had. They did.

By the time his two gallons—plus 8¢ worth—were about burned, darkness had set in and he wondered if he shouldn't find a good spot to park and spend the night. His heavenly impression remained consistent: continue toward home. About that time, way out on a lonely stretch of country road, he came across a hitchhiker.

Tam had a flat policy in this area: *never pick one up!* His dad had been robbed by vagrants and the papers of that day, just as do ours, contained repeated and gruesome stories about what happens to good Samaritans who err in this matter. To his own amazement, however, Tam felt strongly constrained to stop and give this man a lift.

Inquiry revealed his rider was headed for Marion, Ohio, just a short distance beyond Lima. Pressed as to whether he could ride with him all the way to Lima, Tam finally had to explain his embarrassing predicament. His new friend laughed heartily, then explained that he was returning from a brief vacation in Chicago and was only hitchhiking to save money. He said, "I'm not broke! Pull into the next station we come to and we'll gas up!"

In telling of the incident years later, the millionaire of today tells how he often, when headed toward Chicago, pulls into that station in Valparaiso where he ashamedly bought the 8¢ worth of gas, just so he can breathe a silent prayer of gratitude to God and roar a **"Fill 'er up!"** to the attendant.

4. THE POEM:

>O for a faith that will not shrink
>>Tho' pressed by many a foe,
>
>That will not tremble on the brink
>>Of any earthly woe;
>
>That will not murmur nor complain
>>Beneath the chast'ning rod,
>
>But in the hour of grief or pain
>>Will lean upon its God;
>
>A faith that shines more bright and clear
>>When tempests rage without,
>
>That, when in danger, knows no fear,
>>In darkness feels no doubt.
>
>Lord, give me such a faith as this,
>>And then, whate'er may come,
>
>I'll taste e'en now the hallowed bliss
>>Of an eternal home.
>
>>—*William H. Bathurst* (1796-1877)

28. 1. THE PROMISE: *"The Lord upholdeth all that fall, and raiseth up all those that be bowed down. The eyes of all wait upon thee; and thou givest them their meat in due season. Thou openest thine hand, and satisfiest the desire of every living thing"* (Psalm 145:14-16).

2. THE POINT: While there is a sense in which God provides for "every living thing," He has special provision and special enablement for His children who are "bowed down" with heavy cares and seasons of discouragement in the midst of grievous testings. The secret of waiting upon Him is rewarded by ample provision "in due season."

3. THE PROOF: In her book, *Climbing,* the wife of the noted missionary, Jonathan Goforth, tells of visiting in an area of China that had been ravished in the Boxer rebellion, with many missionaries and Christians slaughtered. One of the Swedish missionaries told how she and her husband and several children had been in Stockholm in the Spring of 1900, all set to come back to China, when the Boxer uprising took place and thwarted their plans.

Unfortunately, they had spent almost every penny they had in this world on their outfit and passage back to China, expecting to leave immediately, and there were no funds for the delay-caused living in Sweden. Times were tough, the testing was rough, and the impoverished family found itself subsisting almost entirely on potatoes.

Then the day dawned when the servant girl reported to her missionary mistress and announced that the potato supply had been exhausted. Tears started rolling down the missionary's cheeks as she lamented, "We have no money. We will surely starve!" Then she broke down completely in bitter, convulsive sobbing.

The servant girl gently laid her hand on the broken lady's arm, saying, "Mrs. H., don't cry. This is just an opportunity to see what God can do!"

Immediately the missionary brushed back her tears, determined in her heart she would not allow a little maid to trust God more implicitly than she, and started about her regular duties in the household. All the while she was telling herself, "I will wait on the Lord and see what He can do."

It was at least one hour before lunchtime when a strange man appeared at the door to inquire, "Are you Mrs. H.?"

Replying affirmatively, she was informed by the gentleman that he had just arrived by boat from Finland, where he had heard her husband speak about their work in China. Then he happily announced, "Since I was coming to Stockholm, I thought I would bring a few bags of potatoes for you, thinking you might need them. And I put the half of a sheep along with them!"

The lady ended her story to Mrs. Goforth, rejoicing, "That is the way the Lord deals with me!"

And that is the way He deals with all of His servants who wait upon Him to see what He can do!

4. THE POEM:

If you have gone a little way ahead of me, call back—
'Twill cheer my heart and help my feet along the stony track;
And if, perchance, Faith's light is dim, because the oil is low,
Your call will guide my lagging course as wearily I go.

Call back, and tell me that He went with you into the storm;
Call back, and say He kept you when the forest's roots were torn;
That when the heavens thundered and the earthquake shook the hill,
He bore you up and held you where the very air was still.

O friend, call back and tell me, for I cannot see your face;
They say it glows with triumph, and your feet bound in the race;
But there are mists between us, and my spirit eyes are dim,
And I cannot see the glory, though I long for word of Him.

But if you'll say He heard you when your prayer was but a cry,
And if you'll say He saw you through the night's sin-darkened sky—
If you have gone a little way ahead, O friend, call back—
'Twill cheer my heart and help my feet along the stony track.

29. 1. THE PROMISE: *"The Lord is nigh unto all them that call upon him, to all that call upon him in truth. He will fulfill the desire of them that fear him: he also will hear their cry, and will save them"* (Psalm 145:18,19).

2. THE POINT: God grants "desires"! Indefinite praying is not the secret of effectual intercession. Calling in sincerity includes being specific. Those who "fear" Him, when they "call upon him in truth," have a right to expect their desires fulfilled.

3. THE PROOF: When A. C. Dixon graduated from Wake Forest College, he wrote C. H. Spurgeon and asked permission to enroll in his Pastors' College. Spurgeon refused the request. [*Ironically, Dixon later become one of Spurgeon's successors at the Tabernacle!*] He then decided to pursue studies at the Baptist Theological Seminary at Greenville, South Carolina. However, after preaching all summer on tour with his father, he received a combined call from a country church at Mount Olive, North Carolina, and a church at Bear Marsh—3 or 4 miles from Mount Olive. He was asked to pastor both churches, preaching in each on alternate Sundays. Dixon decided to accept, delaying seminary days for one year in favor of gaining practical experience. It proved to be a blessed decision!

Shortly after he had begun his ministry, Dixon felt burdened to ask God for one hundred souls *saved* and *baptized* during his days on that field. It became his constant daily cry to Heaven. Revival broke out; there were conversions almost every service. Many memorable experiences took place, including a wonderful awakening in nearby Maysville.

On a Sunday morning in September, the youthful minister stood in the pulpit of the Bear Marsh church to preach his farewell message. He was leaving the following day for the seminary at Greenville. With a rejoicing that beggars description, he reviewed in his mind the past nine months of soul winning. But he was also painfully and acutely conscious of the fact that, while many more than a hundred had come to Christ, only ninety-four of this number had followed through with obedience in believer's baptism. At the close of the message, five people responded to the invitation, claiming Christ as Saviour and requesting baptism.

Happily, the young pastor announced that there would be a baptizing that afternoon at Williams' Mill Pond. Since his own clothes were already packed to leave for school, he had to borrow clothes from a deacon for the service. On the way to the pond, he lifted his heart to God and cried, "Dear Lord, thank You for the more than one hundred conversions. Thank You for the ninety-nine who have gone on in requesting baptism. However, I asked for one hundred saved *and baptized.* At this late date I have no idea where the other one is coming from, but I believe Thee and thank Thee again. Furthermore, I promise to tell this story for Thy glory of how wonderfully You answered prayer as long as I live."

When he arrived at the pond he found the candidates and some others waiting for the simple service. Immediately a man stepped up to him and said, "Sir, would you baptize me along with the others?"

Dixon questioned: "Are you a Christian?"

"Yes," he replied, "I gave my heart to Christ last Sunday while you were preaching. I know I am saved."

Testing him, Dixon said: "It is rather late for examination and clothes in which to be baptized. What about that?"

"If you don't mind, sir," the young man responded, "I'll be baptized in my Sunday-go-to-meeting clothes. My wife is one of those waiting to be baptized and I want to be baptized with her." *And he was,* walking the two miles afterward to his home in sopping wet dress clothes.

What a thrilling experience Dixon had to take with him to seminary regarding God's proven power in answering prayer. He had received exactly one hundred souls converted and baptized in answer to his believing intercession. *Exactly* the number he had requested; not one more and not one less!

4. THE POEM:
>Strong Son of God, immortal Love,
>>Whom we that have not seen Thy face,
>>By faith and faith alone, embrace,
>Believing where we cannot prove.
>We have but faith: we cannot know,
>>For knowledge is of things we see;
>>And yet we trust it comes from Thee,
>A beam in darkness: let it grow.
>>>—*Alfred Tennyson* (1809-1892)

30.

1. THE PROMISE: *"Trust in the Lord with all thine heart; and lean not unto thine own understanding. In all thy ways acknowledge him, and he shall direct thy paths"* (Proverbs 3:5,6).

2. THE POINT: Utter abandonment to Christ results in sure, safe leading. When the child of God commits every detail of his life and work to his Redeemer, he can be absolutely confident that his direction will be divinely controlled.

3. THE PROOF: The noted missionary writer, Rosalind Goforth, tells of a remarkable instance of guidance when she and her equally noted husband, Jonathan, were still courting. She was, at the time, engaged in working among the East End slums in Toronto, Canada. She described the incident as follows:

"New Year's Day, 1887, was bitterly cold. Jonathan Goforth and I started for a walk through the Rosedale ravine just north of my home. On reaching Parliament Street, instead of turning northward to the ravine, I stopped short and said, 'Jonathan, I feel strangely impressed that we should go south down to the slum district.'

"He looked at me amazed, and for several moments we stood debating, for he strongly objected, saying very truly that Parliament Street was the last place for a lover's walk!

"At last I said, 'Did you ever feel so clearly led to do something that you just *had* to do it?'

"To this he replied, 'If that is how you feel, let us go south.' (But it was a very silent walk!) For almost a mile and a half we walked down Parliament. Then I led the way a block east. By this time I was getting pretty nervous.

"Hesitating for a moment, I led on down Sackville Street for over a block, then stopped in front of a small cottage and said, 'O Jonathan, don't look at me as if I had gone crazy! Let us knock at this door.'

"Jonathan, evidently getting anxious, exclaimed, 'But why?'

" 'I don't know,' I replied. Now I must say the man of this house was such a drunken fellow I had always avoided visiting his wife at times when he might be in. But at this time I knew of no reason whatever why I should call. We knocked.

"The husband opened the door, and on seeing me cried out, with tears running down his face, *'Oh, Miss Bell-Smith, God has sent you!'*

"We found the place like an ice house: no fuel, no fire, no food. The poor wife was lying on a miserable bed with but little over her and seemingly coughing her life away. In the corner of the room lay a dead baby, born a few hours before. Their sad story was quickly told. The man had gone to the city hall for help, but it was closed, it being New Year's Day. Returning to his wife with his last hope of help gone, he sank down by her bedside and joined her in crying to the Lord to send someone to them. At that very time the strange impelling had come to me."

Mrs. Goforth went on to tell how, forty years later when her daughter, Ruth, was on furlough and addressing a meeting in the East End Mission Hall, an elderly, crippled lady was helped in and seated by the door. At the close of the service, she asked that Ruth be brought to her, unwrapped a tiny parcel containing a small gold coin worth two dollars and fifty cents, and gave it to her, commenting, "Give this to your mother and tell her I have never forgotten how she saved my life forty years ago."

It was the same woman!

4. THE POEM:

The Hand that holds the ocean's depth can hold my small affairs,
The Hand that guides the universe can carry all my cares.
I'm glad I cannot shape my way, I'd rather trust His skill;
I'm glad the ordering is not mine, I'd rather have Thy will.
I do not know the future, and I wouldn't if I might,
For faith to me is better far than faulty human sight.

31.

1. THE PROMISE: *"Commit thy works unto the Lord, and thy thoughts shall be established"* (Proverbs 16:3).

2. THE POINT: Any Christian on praying ground, regardless of the nature of the work involved, can have his thoughts correctly established by God in complete accordance to His will, in answer to believing intercession.

3. THE PROOF: A Christian lady on the West Coast, who had a very responsible position with a large business concern, heard me speak one night on this text. So impressed was she with the tremendous magnitude of the promise that the following morning found her early at her desk, committing that day's labors unto the Lord and earnestly seeking both His wisdom and His enablement.

Strangely, everything seemed to go wrong! For some reason or other she could not get her mind off a government contract she had approved the previous day, but had placed in the outgoing mail basket too late to be picked up that afternoon. Trying desperately now to concentrate on the new figures before her, the thought of that approved, signed and sealed contract prevented completely any efficiency.

Telling me about it later, she said: "I could not understand it. Here I had asked God for His help to do my best and, seemingly,

I was doing my very worst. There was not the slightest doubt in my mind that the contract in question was correct, since I had carefully checked and double-checked the figures before signing. Finally, because I couldn't seem to accomplish anything else, I reluctantly took the contract in question out of the basket, ripped open the envelope, and began the tedious task of rechecking my figures a final time.

"To my utter amazement, I discovered a previously overlooked error in the amount of several thousand dollars. Since it was in favor of the government and against my company, if I had failed to check those figures again it would have cost our organization thousands of dollars. I am **never** going to sit down at my desk again without asking God to establish my thoughts before I start my work!"

4. THE POEM:

He answered prayer: so sweetly that I stand
 Amid the blessings of His wondrous hand
 And marvel at the miracle I see,
The favors that His love hath wrought for me.

Pray on for the impossible, and dare
Upon thy banner this brave motto bear,
 "My Father answers prayer."

32.

1. THE PROMISE: *"He that hath pity upon the poor lendeth unto the Lord; and that which he hath given will he pay him again"* (Proverbs 19:17).

2. THE POINT: God will remain under obligation to no one! When a child of God undertakes to help one less fortunate than himself who is in needy circumstances, our blessed Lord considers it a loan to Himself. And He always pays His debts—WITH EXCELLENT INTEREST!

3. THE PROOF: When the drunken Cornish miner, Billy Bray, got saved in the early 19th century, God received a servant who meant business all of the way and all of the time. Noted for his shouting and praising God—often in the form of a "Davidic dance" in the pulpit—this unlettered trophy of grace exhibited marvelous faith in the promises of God. While his wife, Joey, warned him repeatedly, "We shall be brought to the union [Cornish poorhouse] if you go on in this way," he continued giving "beyond his means" all the while assuring her, "Never mind, my dear Joey, the Lord will provide." And provide He did!

Here is one incident just as Billy told it.

"At one time I had been at work the whole of the month, but had no wages to take up when payday came; and as we had no bread in the house, 'Joey' advised me to go up and ask the 'captain' to lend me a few shillings, which I did, and he let me have ten shillings. On my way home I called to see a family, and found they were worse off than myself; for though we had no bread, we had bacon and potatoes, but they had neither. So I gave them five shillings, and went towards home. Then I called on another family, and found them, if possible, in greater distress than the former. I thought I could not give them less than I had given the others; so I gave them the other five shillings, and went home. And Joey said—

" 'Well, William, have you seen the captain?'

" 'Yes.'

" 'Did you ask him for any money?'

" 'Yes; he let me have ten shillings.'

" 'Where is it?'

" 'I have given it away.'

" 'I never saw the fellow to you in my life. You are enough to try any one.'

" 'The Lord isn't going to stay in my debt very long,' and I then went out. For two or three days after this Joey was mighty down; but about the middle of the week, when I came home from the mine, Joey was looking mighty smiling, so I thought there was something up. Presently Joey said—

" 'Mrs. So-and-so has been here today.'

" 'Oh!'

" 'And she gave me a sovereign [twenty shillings].'

" 'There, I told you the Lord wasn't going to stay in my debt very long; there's the ten shillings, and ten shillings interest.' "

4. THE POEM:

> Not fear or doubting,
>   With Christ on my side,
> I hope to die shouting,
>   "The Lord will provide."

33.

1. THE PROMISE: *"Man's goings are of the Lord; how can a man then understand his own way?"* (Proverbs 20:24).

2. THE POINT: God oversees and overrules in the comings and goings of His own. Carefully directing man's steps—both his starts and his stops—our Lord so manages those activities that man often cannot understand his own way. In it all is God's loving protection.

3. THE PROOF: When Bob Jones College was still located at Cleveland, Tennessee—and Bob Jones University was under construction at its present site in Greenville, South Carolina—the founder, Dr. Bob Jones, Sr., found it necessary to make a trip to Atlanta with regard to some of the building problems they were experiencing. Checking into the huge downtown Winecoff Hotel, he was compelled to phone back to the school's business manager, R. K. "Lefty" Johnson, requesting that he fly down with additional information.

After the business matters were taken care of, Dr. Jones

decided to leave for his next engagement in Mobile, Alabama, a day ahead of schedule. Phoning the hotel where he had reservations, he was told they not only couldn't give him his room a day early, but since a convention was in progress in the city, no other hotel would be able to give him a room either.

Undaunted, Dr. Jones called another hotel where he had frequently stopped, The Battle House, and received the same information. Just as he was about to give up on the idea of an early start to Mobile, the manager at The Battle House told him to come ahead and he would see that he got a room, even if he had to give him his own room for the night.

At first it was decided that Johnson would take the room Jones was releasing at the Winecoff, but finally Dr. Jones decided, very much against Johnson's wishes, that Lefty should return immediately to Cleveland. This meant a long, cold, uncomfortable trip on a bus, taking most of the night.

Ah, but how wonderfully—if not mysteriously—God was moving, His wonders to perform!

That very night, at the Winecoff Hotel, fire broke out on the fifth floor with most of the damage and fatalities coming from the sixth floor—in the very proximity of the room Dr. Jones had occupied and Dr. Johnson had complained because he couldn't occupy. A total of 120 souls perished in that terrible holocaust.

And, but for the merciful grace of God, Dr. Jones or Dr. Johnson would have been numbered among the statistics. Whether the child of God "understands his own way" or not, how good God is!

4. THE POEM:

> For wisely the will of the Lord ordains
> From hour to hour our pleasures and pains;
> The given pain brings a given might,
> The given pleasure yields rare delight.
> In the heart of man 'tis the Spirit's voice
> That crieth ever, "Rejoice! Rejoice!"
> He shall cheerfully, gratefully, joyfully live,
> Who taketh only what God doth give.
>
> —*C. W. Harris*

34.

1. THE PROMISE: *"He that hath a bountiful eye shall be blessed; for he giveth of his bread to the poor"* (Proverbs 22:9).

2. THE POINT: The expression "bountiful eye" is literally "good of eye" and speaks of one who actively seeks those he can help, one who has a benevolent disposition. When God's children recognize they are simply stewards of what God has given, He blesses them in order that they might, in turn, bless others.

3. THE PROOF: Dr. A. J. Gordon was a man with a bountiful eye. On one occasion he related the following incidents which took place within the span of a single day:

"Opening my mail one morning I found a most earnest appeal from a poor student in whom I had for some time taken much interest. He detailed the circumstances by which, in spite of his utmost endeavours, he had been brought into rare straits, debts for board and books severely pressing him, until he was utterly discouraged. He was extremely reluctant to ask aid, and only wrote now, he said, to tell me how earnestly he had besought the Lord for deliverance, and to request my prayers on his behalf. It was only a little sum that he needed to help him out of his difficulties—fifty dollars—but it was a great sum for a poor student, and he was now asking the Lord to send it.

"Having read his letter with real sympathy, I continued opening my mail when, to my surprise, the next letter whose seal I broke was from a wealthy gentleman, expressing great thankfulness for a service I had rendered him a few days before and enclosing a cheque for fifty dollars which he begged me to accept as a token of his gratitude. Instantly I perceived that the poor student's prayers were heard—that the second letter contained the answer to the first; and, endorsing the cheque, I sent it by return mail to the young man, with my congratulations for his speedy deliverance.

"The noon mail of the same day brought another letter of the same sort from another college. A young colored man, full of faith and earnest desire to fit himself for useful service in the Lord's work, had made himself known to me some months before; and, as he had, by his earnest piety and diligent scholarship, approved himself to his teacher, I had done what I could to help him. He now wrote, telling a pathetic story of his struggles, how sparingly he had lived, how he had failed in getting help from expected sources, and how now, having reached the end of the term, he was in debt and nothing to pay. He too had called earnestly upon the Lord, but as yet no help had come. To show me how prudently he had lived he enclosed a list of his expenditures, which demonstrated clearly enough how poorly he had fared.

"Toward night I was at the telegraph office writing a despatch to the poor student to say I would be responsible for one-half of the amount needed, provided he could raise the other half from Mr. W. But what his street number was I could not remember; neither could I recall just the amount needed. So I went back to the house to find his letter in order to get the exact address.

"On my way I called at a certain place to pay a bill—thirty-seven dollars and fifty cents. I had written a cheque for the sum, and as I passed it to the bookkeeper, he turned to look up the account, and said, 'This bill is paid, sir; you do not owe us anything.'

" 'Who paid it?' I enquired.

" 'I cannot say; only I know that it was settled several weeks ago.' And so saying, he handed back my cheque.

"I took it, quite surprised to find myself so much better off than I expected, and returned to my house to find the poor student's letter. Referring to it, I found that, in adding up his little list of debts, it came to just thirty-seven dollars and fifty cents. The Lord had provided the exact amount, even to the cents. I had only to endorse the Lord's cheque again, and sent it forward.

"Mark you, it was not my prayers that were answered, for I had not been moved specially to pray for these young men, not being aware of the necessity. It was not my money; the Lord provided the exact funds in each instance; but I have told you literally what happened. Does not the Lord know how to provide?"

4. THE POEM:

Is thy cruse of comfort wasting? Rise and share it with another;
And through all the years of famine it shall serve thee and thy brother.
Love divine will fill thy storehouse, or thy handful still renew;
Scanty fare for one will often make a royal feast for two.

For the heart grows rich in giving; all its wealth is living grain;
Seeds which mildew in the garner, scattered, fill with gold the plain.
Is thy burden hard and heavy? Do thy steps drag wearily?
Help to bear thy brother's burden; God will bear both it and thee.

Numb and weary on the mountains, wouldst thou sleep amidst the snow?
Chafe that frozen form beside thee, and together both shall glow.
Art thou stricken in life's battle? Many wounded round thee moan;
Lavish on their wounds thy balsams, and that balm shall heal thine own.

Is thy heart a well left empty? None but God its void can fill;
Nothing but a ceaseless fountain can its ceaseless longings still.
Is the heart a living power? Self-entwined its strength sinks low;
It can only live in loving, and, by serving, love will grow.

—*Elizabeth Rundle Charles* (1828-1896)

35.

1. THE PROMISE: *"Foolishness is bound in the heart of a child; but the rod of correction shall drive it far from him"* (Proverbs 22:15).

2. THE POINT: All children are born with a nature of wrath (Ephesians 2:3); they are self-centered (Isaiah 53:6b), deceitful (Psalm 58:3), rebellious (Romans 3:16), and give ample and convincing evidence of their Adamic heritage (Romans 5:19a). How can such be corrected and remedied? By giving proper and adequate discipline!

3. THE PROOF: George R. Stuart, a contemporary of Sam Jones, was just one of the fiery, fervent Methodist evangelists

which the South produced at its spiritual peak. He was at his best in dealing with character development and, when preaching on the home, often told of a mother who raised seven outstanding Christian sons without a single black sheep among them. When asked how she had achieved such success, she would reply: "I did it with prayer and hickory."

One night in Virginia, after a message in which he referred to this incident, a gentleman came up to him, grabbed his hand, and declared with great emotion, "Don't fail, wherever you go, to impress upon your hearers that lady's prayer-and-hickory method."

Going on, he said, "I was the indulgent, pampering father of an only son, badly spoiled and openly rebellious. When the lad was fifteen years old he was expelled from school on two occasions. The second time I was sitting by the fire when my wife came to ask why I hadn't come to bed. I said, 'I can't sleep, thinking about our boy.' Her answer went like a dagger to my heart: 'It is all your fault. Why should you expect others to control him when you never controlled him yourself?' I knew her words were true and they drove me to my knees in heartbroken intercession. I confessed, 'Lord, I am guilty. If You will forgive the past, I will control that boy in the future.'

"After a sleepless night I invited my son to go with me for a walk. We went into the woodland near our house and I cut a good switch from a tree. First I outlined to him the course of his rebellion, then I acknowledged my failure to handle the situation properly heretofore, assuring him that things were going to be different. 'As a matter of fact,' I told him, 'I have brought you out here this morning to punish you for past disobedience.'

"I told him to take off his coat and he defiantly replied, 'I won't.' I looked him straight in the eye and said, 'Son, I am your father; you are my boy. I promised Almighty God last night on my knees that I would control you, and I will either whip you here this morning or one of us will die in this woodland. Now, take off your coat!'

"For the first time in fifteen years he saw the spirit of authority in my eye and he took off his coat. After I had administered the whipping, I said, 'Now get on your knees with me,' and we prayed together. I told God again of my neglect and of my son's waywardness, promising God in my son's presence that I would be faithful to my duty the remainder of my life. Then I asked God's blessing upon the lad. When we arose from our knees, he put his head on my breast and an arm around my neck, and we just wept together for a long time. Then he looked up and said, 'Father, I will never give you any more trouble.'

"From that moment to this one, he has never given me a bit of trouble. He has been the most obedient son a father ever had, or could have. Married now, he is a steward in the Methodist Church and no truer, nobler Christian man walks the earth than my precious son."

Most juvenile delinquency stems from parental deficiency!

4. THE POEM:

> 'Twas a sheep, not a lamb, that strayed away,
>   In the parable Jesus told—
> A grown-up sheep that had gone astray
>   From the ninety and nine in the fold.
>
> Out on the hillside, out in the cold,
>   'Twas a sheep the Good Shepherd sought;
> And back to the flock, safe into the fold,
>   'Twas a sheep the Good Shepherd brought.
>
> And why for the sheep should we earnestly long
>   And as earnestly hope and pray?
> Because there is danger, if they go wrong,
>   They will lead the lambs astray.
>
> For the lambs will follow the sheep, you know,
>   Wherever the sheep may stray;
> When the sheep go wrong, it will not be long
>   Till the lambs are as wrong as they.
>
> And so with the sheep we earnestly plead,
>   For the sake of the lambs, today;
> If the sheep are lost, what terrible cost
>   Some lambs will have to pay!

36.

1. THE PROMISE: *"He that covereth his sins shall not prosper: but whoso confesseth and forsaketh them shall have mercy"* (Proverbs 28:13).

2. THE POINT: Trouble, frustration and defeat will follow the steps of the individual who tries to hide his sin. On the other hand, an honest facing of sin, with its accompanying forsaking and making whatever restitution is necessary, will bring peace, joy and the blessed prosperity of God.

3. THE PROOF: Billy Sunday's father, Pvt. William Sunday, died in the Civil War when Billy was only a month old. The famous evangelist often referred to those early years of life when he "butted and fought and struggled" for everything he got. It was during those days, when he was only fourteen years of age, that he got a job as janitor in a school. He had to rise at two in the morning and fire up fourteen coal stoves, in addition to sweeping the floors. His salary was twenty-five dollars a month.

One month, when he cashed his check at the bank, the teller inadvertantly gave him forty dollars instead of twenty-five. He told a lawyer friend about it and the friend advised him to keep the money. He said, "Don't be a chump. If you were shy ten dollars and you went back you would not get it, and if they hand out fifteen dollars, don't be a fool, keep it." So he did.

He not only kept it, he purchased a new suit with the surplus. It was the first ready-to-wear suit of clothes Sunday had ever owned in his life. However, that was not the end of the story. Here it is in the evangelist's own words:

"Years afterwards I said, 'I ought to be a Christian,' and I got on my knees to pray, and the Lord seemed to touch me on the back and say, 'Bill, you owe that Farmers' Bank fifteen dollars with interest,' and I said, 'Lord, the bank don't know that I got that fifteen dollars,' and the Lord said, 'I know it'; so I struggled along for years, probably like some of you, trying to be decent and honest and right some wrong that was in my life, and every time I got down to pray the Lord would say, 'Fifteen dollars with interest, Nevada, Iowa; fifteen dollars, Bill.' So years afterwards

I sent that money back, enclosed a check, wrote a letter and acknowledged it, and I have the peace of God from that day to this, and I have never swindled anyone out of a dollar."

4. THE POEM:

O for a heart to praise my God, a heart from sin set free,
A heart that always feels Thy blood so freely shed for me!

A heart resigned, submissive, meek, my great Redeemer's throne;
Where only Christ is heard to speak, where Jesus reigns alone.

A humble, lowly, contrite heart, believing, true, and clean,
Which neither life nor death can part from Him that dwells within.

A heart in every thought renewed, and full of love divine;
Perfect, and right, and pure, and good, a copy, Lord, of Thine!

Thy nature, gracious Lord, impart; come quickly from above,
Write Thy new name upon my heart, Thy new, best name of love.
—*Charles Wesley* (1707-1788)

37. 1. THE PROMISE: *"Thou wilt keep him in perfect peace, whose mind is stayed on thee: because he trusteth in thee. Trust ye in the Lord for ever: for in the Lord JEHOVAH is everlasting strength"* (Isaiah 26:3,4).

2. THE POINT: Those who put their faith and confidence in the Lord have peace independent of outward circumstances. They have an everlasting source of strength on which to draw and God's peace which passeth all understanding is their portion at all times—even unto death!

3. THE PROOF: Some years back, before the Communist blood-purge closed the door to China for evangelical missions, a young Chinese lad, who was receiving his education at a mission school, received Christ as his Saviour and determined to follow the Lord in believers' baptism. He immediately wrote a letter to his father, informing him of his decision. Back came a curt

telegram: "COME HOME AT ONCE!"

The angry, indignant father met his son with a torrent of verbal abuse for "taking up with this foreign-devil religion." He ordered his son to return to school and then report back to him on Saturday. If, by then, he had not abandoned his plans for baptism, dire consequences would be forthcoming.

Saturday dawned and the new convert, after begging a few of his student companions to pray both for him and for his father, went to face the music. In contrast to his previous attitude, the parent was quiet and calm. He took the son into the main room of the home and called his attention to the Ancestral Tablets on the shelf. He warned the lad of the danger which might befall their home and the countryside if the son persisted in actions which would provoke those ancestors.

But the boy firmly responded: "Father, if you understood this matter as I understand it, I am sure that you would be willing. Jesus is my Saviour and my Lord. I have promised to follow Him, and I am to be baptized tomorrow."

The angry parent prepared a big box, three feet deep and three feet square, and had two coolies place it on two planks spanning a small river. Placing the boy in the box, the father made one final appeal: "Give up this foreign-devil religion and you will grow to be a successful man, otherwise you will drown."

The son merely smiled and said: "Father, I am not afraid; you can kill this poor body but you cannot kill me. I belong to Jesus. He will take care of me."

The lid of the box was then securely fastened in place, the father retired to the riverbank, and the two coolies stood waiting for the order to send the box crashing into the river. It never came! Soon the father began to tremble, then he ordered the box brought to the bank and uncovered. Taking the boy by the hand, he questioned: "Son, what has come over you? Whenever I have commanded you to do anything you never dared disobey, and now you disobey in the face of death."

The happy convert replied: "Nothing, Father, except that I

now belong to Jesus, and He takes all fear away."

Then the father begged his young son to tell him more about the redemption in Christ. The following morning the boy was baptized and within three months the father, the mother and two other members of the family had received as Lord and Saviour the One who is able to give perfect peace—*even "in the face of death."*

4. THE POEM:
>Light strains of music, soft and low,
>   That break upon a troubled sleep;
>I hear the promise, old and new,
>   "God will His faithful children keep
>   In perfect peace."
>
>It stills the questionings and doubts,
>   The nameless fears that throng the soul;
>It speaks of love unchanging, sure;
>   And evermore its echoes roll
>   "In perfect peace."

38. 1. THE PROMISE: *"For thus saith the high and lofty One that inhabiteth eternity, whose name is Holy; I dwell in the high and holy place, with him also that is of a contrite and humble spirit, to revive the spirit of the humble, and to revive the heart of the contrite ones"* (Isaiah 57:15).

2. THE POINT: Our holy, majestic Lord delights in granting revival. Whenever His people meet His conditions and wait upon Him with broken, contrite and humble hearts, revival is sure to follow. Anything else would be a violation of His nature of holiness.

3. THE PROOF: Charles G. Finney, the noted revivalist of more than a century ago, relates the following in his

autobiography:

"When I was on my way to Rochester, as we passed through a village some thirty miles east of Rochester, a brother minister whom I knew, seeing me on the canal boat, jumped aboard to have a little conversation with me. . . . The Lord gave him a powerful spirit of prayer, and his heart was broken. As he and I prayed together, I was struck with his faith in regard to what the Lord was going to do there. I recollect he would say, 'Lord, I do not know how it is; but I seem to know that Thou art going to do a great work in this city.' The spirit of prayer was poured out powerfully, so much so, that some persons stayed away from the public services to pray, being unable to restrain their feelings under preaching.

"And here I must introduce the name of a man, whom I shall have occasion to mention frequently, Mr. Abel Clary. . . . He had been licensed to preach; but his spirit of prayer was such— he was so burdened with the souls of men—that he was not able to preach much, his whole time and strength being given to prayer. The burden of his soul would frequently be so great that he was unable to stand, and he would writhe and groan in agony. . . . This Mr. Clary continued in Rochester as long as I did, and did not leave it until after I had left. He never, that I could learn, appeared in public, but gave himself wholly to prayer."

The time of the Rochester meeting was 1830 and, in answer to believing intercession, a mighty revival, followed by a sweeping awakening, broke out in that Western New York community and spread throughout the entire area. Before it was finished, 100,000 new converts had united with the New Testament churches of that region.

4. THE POEM:

Revive Thy work, O Lord! Disturb this sleep of death;
Quicken the smoldering embers now by Thine almighty breath.
Revive Thy work, O Lord! Create soul-thirst for Thee;
But hung'ring for the bread of life, oh, may our spirits be!
Revive Thy work, O Lord! Exalt Thy precious Name;
And, by the Holy Ghost, our love for Thee and Thine inflame.

Revive, revive! And give refreshing show'rs;
The glory shall be all Thine own; the blessing shall be ours.

—*Alfred Midlane* (1825-1909)

39.

1. THE PROMISE: *"Is not my word like as a fire? saith the Lord; and like a hammer that breaketh the rock in pieces?"* (Jeremiah 23:29).

2. THE POINT: The power of the living Word of God is able to break down the hardest heart and melt the most icy attitude of indifference toward the wonderful Gospel of Jesus Christ. Indeed, when the dynamic Word is considered, there are truly no impossible cases!

3. THE PROOF: When the noted evangelist, Dwight Lyman Moody, was in Edinburgh, someone pointed out to him the man reputed to be the most difficult case in all that region. In fact, he was the chairman of the Edinburgh Infidel Club. Moody, in his characteristically gracious manner, went and sat down beside the infidel, commenting, "Well, my friend, I am glad to see you at this meeting. Are you concerned about your spiritual welfare?"

He bluntly replied that he didn't believe in any hereafter.

Moody said, "Will you kneel with me and let me pray for you?"

"I don't believe in prayer."

When repeated efforts to get him on his knees failed, Moody knelt alone beside him and prayed earnestly in his behalf. The infidel merely made a big joke of the whole proceedings.

The evangelist and the infidel met numerous times after that. Later, while ministering in the north of Scotland, Moody saw the infidel and went up to him, placing his hand on his shoulder in a fatherly manner, asking as he did: "Hasn't God answered the prayer?"

He answered: "There is no God. I am just the same as I always have been. If you believe in a God, and in getting prayers answered, here is a challenge: *try your hand on me!*"

Within seven months, during meetings at Liverpool, Moody received a letter from the leading lawyer in Edinburgh, telling how the infidel friend had come to Christ. Already, out of an infidel club of thirty men, a total of seventeen had followed the example of their ex-chairman in coming to Christ for salvation.

4. THE POEM:

> **The Spirit breathes upon the Word,**
>   **And brings the truth to sight;**
> **Precepts and promises afford**
>   **A sanctifying light.**
>
> **A glory gilds the sacred page,**
>   **Majestic like the sun,**
> **It gives a light to every age;**
>   **It gives, but borrows none.**
>
> **The hand that gave it still supplies**
>   **The gracious light and heat;**
> **His truths upon the nations rise:**
>   **They rise, but never set.**
>
> **Let everlasting thanks be Thine**
>   **For such a bright display,**
> **As makes a world of darkness shine**
>   **With beams of heavenly day.**
>
> —*William Cowper* (1731-1800)

---

40. 1. THE PROMISE: *"For I know the thoughts that I think toward you, saith the Lord, thoughts of peace, and not of evil, to give you an expected end. Then shall ye call upon me, and ye shall go* *and pray unto me, and I will hearken unto you. And ye shall seek me, and find me, when ye shall search for me with all your heart"* (Jeremiah 29:11-13).

2. THE POINT: Just as Jehovah wanted His best for Israel in bondage at Babylon, so God delights in answering prayer for His people today. And whenever God's people mean business— sincerely and earnestly—mighty power of the mountain-moving variety is unleashed.

3. THE PROOF: In Dr. John R. Rice's book, *Revival Appeals,* he tells this true story from his personal experience:

"In a revival service at Shamrock, Texas, a young woman arose and with sobs and tears told how her husband was unsaved. 'When I want other things, I go after them,' she said, 'and I have decided this morning that I want my husband saved more than anything else in the world.' The next day I went to the home of the young couple for lunch. After the meal, 'Miss Jessie,' as she was commonly known, brought the Bible and said in the presence of her husband, 'Brother Rice, Charles is not a Christian. I want you to read and pray with him now that he will be saved.' We read the Scriptures and I prayed for the young man. I urged upon him his duty and his danger, but he did not trust the Lord. As we rose from the table, the young husband prepared to take his wife to the store where she worked and to go to his own labor. But Miss Jessie said, 'Charles, I am not going to work this afternoon. You tell Mr. Forbis that I will not be there.' Puzzled, and very grave, the young man went to his job. As I departed, the wife said with tears, 'Brother Rice, how could I stand behind a counter, measure goods, sell hose, ribbons or gloves, knowing that my husband is lost and may die at any moment and go to Hell? I must get hold of God today. My husband must be saved!'

"That night when Charles came home, his wife called him to supper. There was only one plate on the table. Somewhat disturbed, the young husband asked no questions. When he wanted to rest in the evening, Miss Jessie said, 'No, Charles, you must go with me to church.' And he did.

"That night I preached the best I could, but Charles did not come. Others were saved, the last pleading verse of the invitation was sung, but he did not come! We stood about afterward and talked and prayed until finally all were gone home but a few. Big Jeff Mankins stood ready to pull the light switch in the tabernacle. The janitor was ready to lock the door. Miss Jessie stood in the center of the floor weeping. When Charles suggested, 'Honey, we had better go,' she simply shook her head and sobbed the more. I saw him walk here and yonder, distressed and troubled, until finally when I laid my hand on his arm, he burst into tears. I will never forget how he came up behind his young wife, put his arms around her and said, 'Jessie, I will settle it tonight!' She won her husband's salvation because she put it first."[1]

4. THE POEM:

>I often say my prayers;
>But do I ever pray?
>And do the wishes of my heart
>Go with the words I say?
>I may as well kneel down
>And worship gods of stone,
>As offer to the living God
>A prayer of words alone,
>For words without the heart
>The Lord will never hear;
>Nor will He to those lips attend
>Whose prayers are not sincere.
>—*John Burton* (1773-1822)

[1] From REVIVAL APPEALS by John R. Rice. Copyright 1945 by Sword of the Lord Publishers, Murfreesboro, Tennessee. Used by permission.

41. 1. THE PROMISE: *"Call unto me, and I will answer thee, and shew thee great and mighty things, which thou knowest not"* (Jeremiah 33:3).

2. THE POINT: Jehovah God invites His people to pray big prayers. For those who call upon Him in faith, He has not only guaranteed to answer, He has promised to perform great feats and mighty works—the kind unknown to ordinary mortals.

3. THE PROOF: They called her "Holy Ann." Born in Ireland and living long in Canada where she served as a maid in the home of Dr. Reid, Ann Preston became known as one "to whom Heaven seemed always open and her well-nigh every petition granted," so powerful was her prayer life. On the Sunday following her funeral, the mayor of Toronto testified in his church: "I have had two honors this week. It has been my privilege to have an interview with the President of the United States. This is a great honor. Then I have been pallbearer to Holy Ann. Of the two honors, I prize the latter most."

In a brief biography of her life, "An Irish Saint," Helen E. Bingham tells of the time, in the dead of winter, the doctor prescribed a diet of fresh eggs and milk. Not a single fresh egg could be found anywhere in the village. Ann, who had been unable to walk for more than a year, began to make the matter a subject of earnest prayer.

Her biographer wrote: "She was sitting in her chair shortly after this, between the kitchen door and the back stairway. The door having been left ajar, to her surprise a hen came in and dropped down at Ann's feet. Something said to her, 'Lift it up and put it on the first step of the stair.' Intuitively Ann recognized that her Father was about to meet her need. The hen went upstairs, and in her simple way Ann asked that it might not be permitted to cackle, lest Dr. Reid's daughters should hear it. (In the village at that time there was another unique character who was the laughingstock of the boys because she permitted the hens to live in her house, and Ann did not want to be likened to old Peggy Casey.) After a few minutes the hen came down very quietly and Ann reached to the door and let her out.

"Then another great difficulty faced her. She had not put any weight on her foot for a long time. It was impossible for her to walk, and while she was confident that the doctor's prescription had been filled at the top of the stairs, she did not know how she was to obtain it. She prayed, and felt that the answer came, 'Go up for it.' But in her simple way she said, 'Father, how can I? It is impossible.'

". . .She worked her chair toward the door, and then, sitting on the first step, she raised herself with her hands, step after step, until she had reached the top. The hen had laid the egg in an old box just at the head of the stair, and she was able to reach it without getting off the top step. . .She then managed to descend in the same fashion, and was just safely back in her chair when Paddy, the servant, walked in. Ann prayed, 'Now, Father, don't let him ask me where I got it,' and in response to her simple faith he took the egg without a word and fixed it for her without making any inquiry. This is the more surprising when it is stated that he had been all through the village in his endeavor to secure eggs for Ann.

"For three weeks the hen returned every day without making the slightest noise. At the end of this time the doctor one morning said she did not need any more milk and eggs, and recommended beef tea instead."

That very day the hen was discovered in the house by one of the young ladies, was shooed out into the yard and never returned. When Ann hesitated for considerable time to relate this answer to prayer, she sensed God reproving her: "I fed you just as really as I fed Elijah through the ravens, and yet you are ashamed to make it known." The first time she tried to tell the story, the lady to whom she spoke refused to believe it. Ann said, "Well, my Father will make you believe it before I go," and a wonderful answer to prayer regarding money for her return trip convinced the skeptic.

4. THE POEM:
>O God of Bethel! By whose hand
>>Thy people still are fed;
>Who, through this weary pilgrimage
>>Hast all our fathers led—
>Our vows, our prayers we now present
>>Before Thy throne of grace:

>God of our fathers! Be the God
>   Of their succeeding race.
>
>Through each perplexing path of life,
>   Our wandering footsteps guide;
>Give us each day our daily bread,
>   And raiment fit provide.
>Oh, spread Thy covering wings around,
>   Till all our wand'rings cease,
>And at our Father's loved abode,
>   Our souls arrive in peace.
>
>Such blessings from Thy gracious hand,
>   Our humble prayers implore;
>And Thou shalt be our chosen God
>   And portion evermore.
>
>   —*John Logan*

42.

1. THE PROMISE: *"I will give them one heart, and I will put a new spirit within you; and I will take the stony heart out of their flesh, and will give them an heart of flesh: That they may walk in my statutes, and keep mine ordinances, and do them: and they shall be my people, and I will be their God"* (Ezekiel 11:19,20).

2. THE POINT: While the reference is to the transformation Israel will experience at the coming of Christ in glory, the words nonetheless describe the reality of every sinner who comes to Christ for salvation. He immediately receives a new heart, becomes a new creature, and experiences a new life. It is the most remarkable, most miraculous transformation known to man.

3. THE PROOF: The late Gipsy Smith, during his early ministry with the Salvation Army in England, was sent by his superiors to minister at Newcastle. One of the local ruffians who attended the service was a hard, tough hombre whom his mates

called "Bricky." He and his companions did not come to worship, they came to sneer and scoff.

"The Gipsy," as he was called in those days, spotted him in the crowd and went to speak privately to him. Bricky responded nonchalantly, "I am a good churchman. I say my prayers every night."

Smith queried, "Do you know the Lord's Prayer?"

"Of course I do!"

"Let's hear it, then."

Bricky started out intoning, "The Lord is my shepherd; I shall not want," etc.

The kindly evangelist dealt with him at length, but seemingly was unable to get through to him. He kept returning to the meetings, however, and he came without his sneering companions. As time progressed, Bricky sensed more and more the awful load of sin he was carrying, along with the mighty, matchless invitations of Christ for forgiveness and cleansing.

One happy night he surrendered to Christ and immediately became a new creation. Smith said: "He was changed from a drunken, swearing, gambling sot into a new creature, and was used as an instrument for the salvation of many others."

Not too many weeks after his conversion—in fact, he was on his way to church at the time—he went by a theater where he used to spend many frivolous hours. His passing was timed in exactness with a large number of his former cronies, on their way into the infamous den.

They said: "Hey, Bricky, where have you been? We haven't seen you for a long time. Are you coming tonight?"

The new convert replied, "No, I cannot. I am serving a new Master."

"Oh," one in the group responded, not understanding what he meant. "But have you seen the transformation scene this year?"

"No," said Bricky, "I have not seen it, but I have felt it."

Ah, this sums it up exactly!

4. THE POEM:

> Fierce was the wild billow, dark was the night,
> Oars labored heavily, foam glimmered white;
> Mariners trembled, peril was nigh;
> Then said the God of gods, "Peace, it is I!"
>
> Jesus, Deliverer! come Thou to me;
> Soothe Thou my voyaging over life's sea;
> Thou, when the storm of death roars sweeping by,
> Whisper, O Truth of Truth, "Peace, it is I!"
>
> —*St. Anatolius, Bishop of Constantinople* (5th Century)

43. 1. THE PROMISE: *"Therefore also now, saith the Lord, turn ye even to me with all your heart, and with fasting, and with weeping, and with mourning: And rend your heart, and not your garments, and turn unto the Lord your God: for he is gracious and merciful, slow to anger, and of great kindness, and repenteth him of the evil"* (Joel 2:12,13).

2. THE POINT: While these words were originally addressed to Judah, they nonetheless constitute the manner of God's mighty mercy in dealing with His own. Whenever the people of God honestly and sincerely face their sins with heart-searching, weeping, fasting and full confession, the One who is "gracious and merciful, slow to anger, and of great kindness" will turn from the impending chastisement and grant blessing in its stead.

3. THE PROOF: The first few years after the Mayflower had deposited her weary pilgrims upon our New England shores were difficult and dangerous, indeed. Of all the crises they faced, however, none was more severe or vital than the drought of mid-1623. With their essential corn crop in the ground and life depending upon its harvest at maturity, a major catastrophe was

in the making. The historian, John Brown, in his *The Pilgrim Fathers of New England,* says: "The younger maize plants began to wither, and the older to mature abortively. Even before the time of harvest, famine began to play havoc among them, and Winslow tells us that he saw men staggering at noonday for want of food. We read, too, of William Brewster sitting down to table with a meagre wooden platter of boiled clams and a pot of water before him. Nevertheless, the grand old spirit was in him still, for over this lenten fare he gave thanks to God that he and his were permitted to 'suck of the abundance of the seas, and of the treasures hid in the sand.' "

After about seven weeks of the terrible drought, which began in early June, Brown tells us: "As day after day the burning sun of July glared down upon their fields, they thought it good that not only should every man privately examine his own estate between God and his conscience, but that also publicly and solemnly they should together humble themselves before the Lord by fasting and prayer. Weaklings neither in work nor worship, these religious exercises continued for eight or nine hours without intermission. In succession they recalled the promises of God, wrestled in prayer, and exhorted each other to steadfastness. They pleaded that the Lord would grant the request of their troubled souls, if their continuance there might in any way stand with His glory and their good. They have left it on grateful record that God was as ready to hear as they to ask. For though when they met in the morning the heavens were still cloudless, and the drought as likely as ever to continue, when they came out of the fort after those hours of pleading supplication, they began to look at each other as only men can look who have been nigh to perishing, and now at last see that rescue is near. For as they wended their way down the hillside the clouds were steadily gathering along the face of the sky, and before many hours were past the rain began to fall in softening showers upon the parched fields. Day after day it continued to fall, till 'it was hard to say whether their withered corn or their drooping affections were most revived.' "

The initial Thanksgiving Day in America came as the result of this victorious answer to prayer!

4. THE POEM:

> Lord, what a change within us one short hour
> Spent in Thy presence, will prevail to make!
> What heavy burdens from our bosoms take,
> What parched grounds refresh, as with a shower!
> We kneel, and all around us seems to lower;
> We rise, and all, the distant and the near,
> Stands forth in sunny outline, brave and clear.
>
> We kneel how weak, we rise how full of power!
> Why, therefore, should we do ourselves this wrong,
> Or others, that we are not always strong;
> That we are ever overborne with care;
> That we should ever weak or heartless be,
> Anxious or troubled; when with us is prayer,
> And joy and strength and courage are with Thee?
>
> —*Archbishop Richard Chenevix Trench* (1807-1886)

44.

1. THE PROMISE: *"The Lord is slow to anger, and great in power, and will not at all acquit the wicked: the Lord hath his way in the whirlwind and in the storm and the clouds are the dust of his feet"* (Nahum 1:3).

2. THE POINT: While Jehovah takes vengeance upon evil doers, His great power overrrules exactly how it is done. In the process, He causes even nature to perform His will and accomplish His work. Whirlwinds, storms—yea, and even clouds—are used to bring about the desired end.

3. THE PROOF: A truly remarkable instance of God's overruling—man proposing, God disposing—came out of World War II. The inimitable Paul Harvey, conservative newscaster,

described the incident as follows:

"It was out there somewhere from an island named Guam that one of our then mightiest bombers took off—a B-29. Another swift, deadly arrow of destruction was on its way—the target, Japan. The sleek bomber turned in a lazy arc above the cloud that shrouded the target for half an hour—three quarters of an hour—fifty-five minutes—until the gas supply would not stand for more of this. It seemed a shame to be right over the primary target of Kokura and then pass it up, but there was no choice. That strange cloud, almost like an omen, said, 'This city must be spared.' With one more puzzled look back, the crew headed for the secondary target. The sky was clear—'Bombs away!' and the B-29 high-tailed it for home.

"Weeks later Major Sweeney received information from military intelligence which made his blood run cold. Those allied prisoners of war, thousands of them, the biggest concentration of imprisoned Americans in enemy hands, had been moved on August 1 to a town named Kokura.

" 'Thank God,' breathed the skipper, 'Thank God for that cloud.'

"Yes, the city which was hidden from our bomber that August 8 was a prison camp and thousands of Americans are now alive who would have died but for that unexplained cloud which rolled in from a sunlit sea. You see, the secondary target that day was Nagasaki, the missile intended for Kokura was the world's second atomic bomb."

4. THE POEM:

I sing the mighty power of God, That made the mountains rise;
That spread the flowing seas abroad, And build the lofty skies.
I sing the wisdom that ordained The sun to rule the day;
The moon shines full at His command, And all the stars obey.

I sing the goodness of the Lord, That filled the earth with food;
He formed the creatures with His word, And then pronounced them good.
Lord, how Thy wonders are displayed, Where'er I turn my eye:
If I survey the ground I tread, Or gaze upon the sky!

There's not a plant or flower below, But makes Thy glories known;

And clouds arise, and tempests blow, By order from Thy throne;
While all that borrows life from Thee Is ever in Thy care,
And everywhere that man can be, Thou, God, art present there.

—*Isaac Watts* (1674-1748)

---

45. 1. THE PROMISE: *"Bring ye all the tithes into the storehouse, that there may be meat in mine house, and prove me now herewith, saith the Lord of hosts, if I will not open you the windows of heaven, and pour you out a blessing, that there shall not be room enough to receive it"* (Malachi 3:10).

2. THE POINT: From a strictly practical standpoint, it pays to tithe. The tithe belongs to God and it is to the Christian's own advantage to be honest with Him in regard to finances. Blessings abundant follow integrity in stewardship.

3. THE PROOF: A few years ago I was out soul winning with a businessman who was serving as chairman of the publicity committee in one of my crusades. He had only been saved a few years at that time and he delighted in relating some of his early trials and blessings. He described how, on one occasion shortly after his conversion, his business was $120,000 in the red. He walked the floor of his home at night, unable to sleep, and days his nerves were ragged and jumpy.

Then one day, driving down the highway listening to a radio preacher, the thought struck him that he was also a debtor to God. Pulling his automobile over to the side of the highway, he bowed his head and promised the Lord he would commence tithing.

Turning to me with a broad smile highlighting his countenance, he said, "In six months' time we were above board!"

If you are in debt, even if for no other reason than that it is a wise business policy, you ought to begin paying your obligations to God *first*.

4. THE POEM:

> Jehovah-jireh, can it mean,
> My all upon Him I can lean?
> Never fear, but trust Him when
> My earthly stores have reached an end?
> Yes, Jehovah-jireh *can* be tried!
> Jehovah-jireh *will* provide!
>
> —*Robert L. Sumner*

46. 1. THE PROMISE: *"And why take ye thought for raiment? Consider the lilies of the field, how they grow; they toil not, neither do they spin: And yet I say unto you, That even Solomon in all his glory was not arrayed like one of these. Wherefore, if God so clothe the grass of the field, which today is, and tomorrow is cast into the oven, shall he not much more clothe you, O ye of little faith?"* (Matthew 6:28-30).

2. THE POINT: If God takes such pains for perfection with minor matters, how much more will He care for the majors! The omnipotent God, who arrays lilies with greater glory and splendor than Solomon on his finest day, will surely provide the clothing needed by His own dear children.

3. THE PROOF: It was the Autumn of 1857. The famous missionary, J. Hudson Taylor, had been in China barely four years. Because of differences over finances—they were operating on "borrowed" money and he believed in trusting God for provision—Taylor had severed his connections with the Chinese Evangelization Society and now had no one behind him but God. Further, he had fallen in love with a lovely, 20-year-old orphan,

Maria Dyer, and wanted to make her his wife. Thwarted by the lady in whose charge she was, he had written to Miss Dyer's legal guardian in England, an uncle, requesting permission to marry.

While in the agony of waiting the four months such an exchange of correspondence would take in those days, a fellow missionary, the Rev. John Quarterman of the American Presbyterian Mission North, was seriously plagued with a case of virulent smallpox. Although Taylor was just recovering from an illness of his own at the time and was in a weakened condition, he volunteered to nurse the patient, doing so until Quarterman died. In the process, he contracted the disease, although a recent vaccination helped him escape with only a mild case.

When the smallpox affair was over, Taylor was compelled to destroy his clothing. He had an empty checkbook and an empty wardrobe, although he would have had more than enough money for clothing had he not been sharing his funds with one fellow missionary and had loaned a sizable amount to another.

Meeting Taylor's needs was a simple matter for his Lord. It was at that precise moment that a long lost box of his clothing, which he had left at Swatow fifteen months previously, put in its unexpected arrival and supplied him with exactly what he needed! He wrote of this miracle, calling it "as appropriate as it was remarkable, and brought a sweet sense of the Father's own providing." No wonder he wrote in his journal: "I would not, if I could, be otherwise than as I am—entirely dependent upon the Lord, and used as a channel to help others." He delighted to walk by faith and not by sight!

4. THE POEM:

>   **Sparrow, He guardeth thee;**
> **Never a flight but thy wings He upholdeth;**
> **Never a night but thy rest He enfoldeth;**
>   **Safely He guardeth thee.**
>
>   **Lily, He robeth thee;**
> **Though thou must fade, by the Summer bemoaned,**
> **Thou art arrayed, fair as monarch enthroned,**
>   **Spotless, He robeth thee.**
>
>   **Hear, thou of little faith:**

> Sparrow and lily are soulless and dying;
> Deathless art thou, will He slight thy faint crying?
> Trust, thou of little faith!
>
> —*Robert Gilbert Welsh*

47.

1. THE PROMISE: *"But seek ye first the kingdom of God, and his righteousness; and all these things shall be added unto you"* (Matthew 6:33).

2. THE POINT: God's people are to put His business FIRST, always. The spiritual ever takes precedence over the material, as the context shows. When we do this, we have His guarantee that He will provide the necessities in the material realm.

3. THE PROOF: When I was with the Baptist church at Boomer, West Virginia, the people were facing some immediate financial burdens. In a letter received shortly after the meeting, the pastor, Bill Tate, a long-time friend, wrote: "This was a blessing to me and I want to share it with you. I mentioned when you were here that we needed $10,000 to pay remaining bills for our new building. We needed it by the first of May—or at least the promise of it.

"After your first message on Monday concerning soul winning, I promised the Lord I wouldn't be concerned about the money, would not even mention it, but would just put soul winning first as never before. On Wednesday after your meeting, I had the promise of $9,000 worth of bonds and $500 from another source. I told the Lord I would, by faith, personally take $500. As it turned out, we needed $9,500. We had it all and all bills are paid! God is so good!"

4. THE POEM:

> Why shouldst thou fill today with sorrow
> About tomorrow,

> My heart?
> One watches all with care most true,
> Doubt not that He will give thee too
> Thy part.
>
> —*Paul Flemming*

48. 1. THE PROMISE: *"Take therefore no thought for the morrow: for the morrow shall take thought for the things of itself. Sufficient unto the day is the evil thereof"* (Matthew 6:34).

2. THE POINT: Our Lord has assured His own—limited, of course, to those in the light of the context who are seeking first His kingdom and His righteousness—that He will meet each day's needs as they arise. Because of this, there is no cause for anxiety regarding the provision, nor setting aside of reserves to meet unforeseen emergencies.

3. THE PROOF: Bristol's George Muller, the miracle man who performed such heroic feats of faith in the nineteenth century, believed and practiced a hand-to-mouth (God's hand to his mouth) existence, refusing to even *accept* contributions from donors for future use. He followed this faith principle in every area of his life and ministry—both spiritual and material—even to the extent of refusing any form of insurance. His influence caused many others to likewise consider the system of insuring as unscriptural.

Their faith was rewarded in some highly remarkable ways. For example, he wrote about one friend: "Received 5 pounds and 10 shillings from a donor who has sent to me for nearly thirty years, as a donation for the Institution, what he would have paid to insurance companies, and who has been many times preserved from fire when it has been near his premises. He writes with this donation: 'There has been another fierce fire within fifty yards of the back of my works and warehouse, a large factory having been completely burnt down in broad daylight. To God be all the praise for His gracious preservation of premises, insured with Himself through our Lord and Saviour, Jesus Christ."

Under date of September 5, 1879, Mr. Muller recorded a gift of 5 pounds from a donor who lived at Newcastle-on-Tyne. With the gift was the comment from the contributor: "Annual thank-offering for protection from fire, and instead of insurance. A great fire was a short time ago on my left, next door but one. House and shop gutted next door to me. My shop free. A few years ago a fire next door on my right. Two smoldering fires at different times discovered on the premises, fires all around; but the Lord Himself, a wall of fire round about me. Blessed be the name of the Lord!"

4. THE POEM:

> He does not lead me year by year nor even day by day.
> But step by step my path unfolds; my Lord directs my way.
>
> Tomorrow's plans I do not know, I only know this minute;
> But He will say, "This is the way, by faith now walk ye in it."
>
> And I am glad it is so. Today's enough to bear;
> And when tomorrow comes, His grace shall far exceed its care.
>
> What need to worry then, or fret? The God who gave His Son
> Holds all my moments in His hand and gives them, one by one.
>
> —*Barbara C. Ryberg*

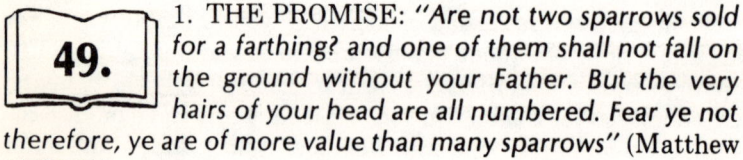

49.

1. THE PROMISE: *"Are not two sparrows sold for a farthing? and one of them shall not fall on the ground without your Father. But the very hairs of your head are all numbered. Fear ye not therefore, ye are of more value than many sparrows"* (Matthew 10:29-31).

2. THE POINT: From a monetary standpoint of view, few

things of earth are worth less than a sparrow. Yet the child of God is assured that the Heavenly Father is vitally interested in a sparrow's fall and, since this is true, how much more He is concerned with every aspect of the believer's life, even the number of hairs on his head! What watchfulness, what protection, what care He therefore manifests in and over His own!

3. THE PROOF: Did you ever "praise God" for continued, repeated interruptions caused by "wrong numbers"? Yet are they not part of the "all things" for which the believer is to give thanks?

In the Eagle Rock section of Los Angeles a number of years ago, the telephone rang in the home of the late Keith L. Brooks. His wife, who was out in the back yard at the time, rushed into the house to answer it.

It was a wrong number!

Mrs. Brooks had just gotten back out into the yard when the phone began to ring incessantly again. Once more she raced through the house to the phone and, once again, it was a wrong number. Apparently it was the same lady who had dialed erroneously moments before.

Would you believe that as soon as Mrs. Brooks returned to the yard the telephone began ringing again with a third wrong number? However, this time as Mrs. Brooks raced through the house, she glanced toward a bedroom and saw smoke and blinding flashes erupting from an electric lamp. She screamed for Dr. Brooks; he ran into the room, yanked the lamp plug from the wall socket and a catastrophe was averted. If his wife had not been called into the house at exactly that moment, tremendous fire damage could easily have resulted.

What "foolish" individual dialed the same wrong number three straight times? We do not know. . .but we do know "why." As Jeremiah 10:23 tells us, "O Lord, I know that the way of man is not in himself: it is not in man that walketh to direct his steps."

4. THE POEM:

He's helping me now—this moment,
   Though I may not see it or hear,
Perhaps by a friend far distant,
   Perhaps by a stranger near,
Perhaps by a spoken message,
   Perhaps by the printed word;
In ways that I know and know not
   I have the help of the Lord.

He's keeping me now—this moment,
   However I need it most
Perhaps by a single angel,
   Perhaps by a mighty host,
Perhaps by the chain that frets me,
   Or the walls that shut me in;
In ways that I know and know not,
   He keeps me from harm and sin.

He's guiding me now—this moment,
   In pathways easy or hard,
Perhaps by a door wide open,
   Perhaps by a door fast barred,
Perhaps by a joy withholden,
   Perhaps by a gladness given;
In ways that I know and know not,
   He's leading me up to Heaven.

He's using me now—this moment,
   And whether I go or stand,
Perhaps by a plan accomplished,
   Perhaps when He stays my hand,
Perhaps by a word in season,
   Perhaps by a silent prayer,
In ways that I know and know not,
   His labor of love I share.[1]

—*Annie Johnson Flint* (1857-1932)

[1] Copyright by Evangelical Publishers, Toronto, Canada. Used by permission.

50.

1. THE PROMISE: *"If ye have faith as a grain of mustard seed, ye shall say unto this mountain, Remove hence to yonder place; and it shall remove; and nothing shall be impossible unto you. Howbeit this kind goeth not out but by prayer and fasting"* (Matthew 17:20,21).

2. THE POINT: The power of faith is limitless and unfathomable. Faith as microscopic as a mustard seed ("which indeed is the least of all seeds," Matthew 13:32), because it has life, can perform incredible feats illustrated by moving mountains or casting sycamine trees into the sea (Luke 17:6). The secret to such faith lies in prayer and fasting, thereby getting the "green light" from God for the action.

3. THE PROOF: In one of his sermons Dr. Richard H. Harvey tells a fascinating story of an incident which took place during his senior year in college. One of the chemistry professors, a Dr. Lee, was a blatant infidel who seemed to feel that one of his principal callings in life was to destroy the faith of his students in God and the Bible. He had a standard lecture belittling prayer, filled with sarcasm and biting humor, he used annually just before classes were dismissed for the Thanksgiving holiday. For 15 years he had used the speech, always ending with a challenge for any student who still believed in prayer to pray that a two-quart glass flask would not break when he dropped it onto the concrete floor.

No one dared accept the challenge! No one, that is, until Harvey's final year in pre-med when a freshman arrived on the campus who was out and out for Jesus Christ.

Since the event was so well publicized—actually, many if not all of the students looked forward to it—the freshman knew well in advance what was coming. He inquired around, found that there was at least one other student on campus who professed to be born again, then went to where Harvey was living.

Explaining that God had shown him He wanted him to accept the professor's challenge, he said his heart had been impressed with the promise that "if two of you shall agree on earth as touching *any thing that they shall ask,* it shall be done" (Matthew 18:19). He asked Harvey to join him in claiming the promise and together they went to the Throne of Grace, beseeching the Heavenly Father for help. During the next two or three weeks, until the hour for the lecture arrived, both young men prayed continuously.

True to the advance billing, Dr. Lee spent his entire lecture hour ridiculing God and the Bible, placing his major emphasis on the matter of prayer. Summing it up, he brought out his glass flask, explaining how it would break into hundreds of pieces if he were to drop it on the concrete floor—*all the prayers of any number of Christian people notwithstanding.*

Dramatically he faced the 300 or so students and asked, "Now, is there any student here who still believes in prayer?" And just as dramatically the freshman believer jumped to his feet and said, "Yes, sir! I do, Dr. Lee."

After taking time to explain it all again and asking several times if the youth still wanted to go through with it, he finally said to the class, sarcasm dripping from every syllable, "Everyone be reverent now while this young man prays."

The bold believer simply lifted his eyes Heavenward and said, "Dear Heavenly Father, in the name of Jesus, I thank You that You have heard me. For Your honor and Christ's name's sake and for the honor of Your servant who puts his trust in You, don't let this flask break. Amen."

The professor then held out the flask, opened his hand and let it crash to the floor. Instead of falling straight down, however, God drew it in so that it struck the toe of Dr. Lee's shoe first, then rolled over.

It remained perfectly intact!

The class gave the professor the horselaugh, the Word of God was vindicated, and a voice for infidelity was put to silence. Dr. Lee never again, as long as he remained at the college, used his lecture on prayer.

In fact, on campus, they still tell the story of the flask that wouldn't break!

4. THE POEM:

> Dare to be a Daniel, dare to stand alone!
> Dare to have a purpose firm! dare to make it known!
>
> Standing by a purpose true, heeding God's command,
> Honor them, the faithful few! All hail to Daniel's Band!
>
> Many mighty men are lost, daring not to stand,
> Who for God had been a host, by joining Daniel's Band!
>
> Many giants, great and tall, stalking thro' the land,
> Headlong to the earth would fall, if met by Daniel's Band!
>
> Hold the gospel banner high! On to vict'ry grand!
> Satan and his host defy, and shout for Daniel's Band!
>
> —*Philip Paul Bliss* (1838-1876)

51.

1. THE PROMISE: *"Again I say unto you, That if two of you shall agree on earth as touching any thing that they shall ask, it shall be done for them of my Father which is in heaven. For where two or three are gathered together in my name, there am I in the midst of them"* (Matthew 18:19,20).

2. THE POINT: Our Lord has given special encouragement for group praying. While husbands and wives have found this promise especially thrilling, it is exceedingly valuable for church prayer meetings, as the context implies. But whenever ANY two saints—seeking the will of God together—are burdened by the "present" Christ to seek the same request, it is something that "shall be done."

3. THE PROOF: Dr. John R. Rice, in that classic on the subject, *PRAYER—Asking and Receiving,* tells of a crusade he and another young preacher conducted in a rural church near Decatur, Texas, back in 1921—shortly after surrendering to

preach. It was a cold, backslidden congregation that had seen no one saved in years.

After seven full days of fruitless labor, the young preachers announced a day of prayer and fasting for the Lord's Day. Only five—the two evangelists, a visiting minister and his wife, and one deacon—stayed after the morning service to fast and pray; all the others went home to a big Sunday dinner "with all the trimmings."

About thirty people assembled at three for an afternoon service and Rice suggested they pray for definite things. One dear, timid lady—after all the others had acknowledged that they had no requests—meekly said, "I would like to see one soul saved tonight, but I have no assurance that I shall." After considerable discussion, during which the visiting minister rebuked the young evangelists for expecting to see people saved in such a backslidden church, Rice and his companion publicly agreed to claim God's promises for the conversion of at least ten souls in the evening service. They solemnly shook hands on it.

Again the visiting preacher publicly rebuked them. One man got his hat and walked out, mumbling, "If God saves ten souls here tonight, I'll never do another wrong thing as long as I live."

After spending the rest of the day in prayer and waiting on God, the young preachers began the evening service. A great crowd came to see if God would answer prayer and not all could get inside the building. After a brief song service and a gospel sermon, the invitation was started. The first to respond was a local bootlegger and gambler named Jernigan, a drunken and profane man. Next was a nineteen-year-old son of one of the members. The two sons of the man who had left the afternoon service muttering were saved. Heaven came down and the people kept coming. When the blessed service finally came to a close, the new converts lined up across the front of the little country church: A TOTAL OF TWENTY-THREE!

4. THE POEM:
>**The God that stopped the sun on high,**
>**And sent the manna from the sky,**

Laid flat the walls of Jericho,
And put to flight old Israel's foe,
Why can't He answer prayer today,
And drive each stormy cloud away?
He turned the water into wine,
And healed the helpless cripple's spine,
Commanded tempests, "Peace, be still,"
And hungry multitudes did fill.
His power is just the same today,
So why not trust Him, watch and pray?
He conquered in the lions' den;
Brought Lazarus back to life again;
He heard Elijah's cry for rain,
And freed the sufferers from pain.
If He could do those wonders then,
Let's prove our mighty God again.
Why can't the God who raised the dead,
Gave youthful David, Goliath's head,
Cast out the demons with a word,
And sees the fall of each wee bird,
Do signs and miracles today?
In that same good, old-fashioned way?
He can! He's just the same today.

—*Martin Luther* (1483-1546)

52. 1. THE PROMISE: *"Come ye after me, and I will make you to become fishers of men"* (Mark 1:17).

2. THE POINT: The secret of developing into an effective, successful winner of souls is found in following Christ. Fruitful fishers are not born, they are "made" by the Master! Imitators of His compassion and concern for souls have the definite, dogmatic guarantee, "I will make you."

3. THE PROOF: One of the finest soul winners this country has ever known, a Baptist layman who called himself "The

Shepherd's Dog," was living proof of our Lord's promise. "Uncle John" Vassar went to the front lines to witness for Christ during the Civil War and an army chaplain, Rev. J. H. Twitchell, described his activities:

"From a merely physical point of view his achievement was prodigious. He began his day at roll-call, and was in a state of intense activity from sixteen to eighteen hours. He ate little and slept little, yet never flagged, and never gave out. Week after week, and seven days in the week, the same even high rate of energy was sustained. I suppose there are very few of the eight thousand officers and men of our division with whom in the time he was with us he did not talk, and with the majority of them more than once or twice. I used to see him running in his eagerness to get about. Yet he was as far as possible from being in a flurry. His restlessness was wholly external. He always knew exactly what he was after. His objects were distinctly before him.

"Conversing with from seventy-five to a hundred different men a day, he came to the fiftieth or sixtieth just as fresh in his manner, just as much interested, just as tender, as at the first. He wasted no words. He went right to the heart of his errand at once, and his bearing was such that it was hardly possible to take offence. . .

"Such a ministry could not fail to be fruitful. Upon hundreds, probably upon thousands, of men he made his mark for eternity. Dear old man! How he loved and how he was loved for Christ's sake! There were joy and sorrow in all hearts when he parted from us. And when, as we were met together in our log chapel the evening after he bade us good-by, one of our soldiers—a Methodist—prayed in stentorian tones, 'O Lord, we thank Thee for sending dear Uncle John Vassar to us, and may God bless him wherever he goes,' a chorus of amens responded, and I saw the tears falling on many a rugged cheek. It is my conviction that few more gracious spirits have been given to the church of Christ in any age than he. The last day alone will reveal how much good he did."

4. THE POEM:
>The Master said, "Come, follow"—
> That was all.
>Earth's joys grew dim,
> My soul went after Him;
>I rose and followed—
> That was all.
>Will you not follow if you hear His call?[1]

[1] From UNCLE JOHN VASSAR or THE FIGHT OF FAITH by Thomas E. Vassar. Copyright, 1931. Reprinted by permission of the American Tract Society, Oradell, New Jersey.

53.

1. THE PROMISE: *"Therefore I say unto you, What things soever ye desire, when ye pray, believe that ye receive them, and ye shall have them"* (Mark 11:24).

2. THE POINT: Two vital and essential characteristics of truly effective prayer are EARNESTNESS and FAITH. The child of God need expect no sensational answers to his intercession if insincerity or unbelief are entwined among the petitions. On the other hand, honest desire and believing confidence comprise a positive guarantee of success!

3. THE PROOF: In Leon McBeth's *The First Baptist Church of Dallas,* he tells of a major problem during the early years of W. A. Criswell's ministry, and how that difficulty was solved. The problem had to do with the tremendous scarcity of parking—especially during weekdays—around the vicinity of the big downtown church. A valuable piece of property nearby became available which the church could obtain for $260,000. Criswell thought it should be purchased immediately, before some business concern snapped it up. The deacons, understandably awed by a current indebtedness of more than a million dollars, refused to go along with the pastor's recommendation.

What happened next, told in Criswell's own words, was as follows: "I stood there looking at the property with Billy Souther, lamenting and grieving that we could not have it. How I wanted and needed it, and how I lamented to think we were going to lose it. Then Billy said to me, 'Pastor, why don't you ask God for it?' 'Ask God for it! Why I've already asked the deacons!' Then I said, 'Billy, I believe I will ask God for it.' And I did. For weeks I was often on my knees asking God for the property. Then one day Mrs. Minnie Slaughter Veal called me on the phone. She said, 'Pastor, I hear you have been down on your knees asking God for a piece of property. Where is it and how much do they want for it?' I told her it would take about $260,000.00. She said, 'Pastor, you go buy it, and I will pay for it.' And she did."

There was a very interesting sequel to the story, by the way. After Mrs. Veal had given the money and the property had been purchased, she called to inquire from Dr. Criswell as to *why* he wanted the property—*she didn't know!* When he explained the details about the proposed parking and recreation building, she became so enthused that she offered to pay for the construction as well! Altogether, Mrs. Veal invested $1,755,500 in this project which did not cost the First Baptist Church a single penny.

4. THE POEM:

>Prayer
>Is asking
>A God
>Who replies.
>
>Prayer
>Is seeking
>For fire
>From the skies.
>
>Prayer
>Is knocking
>Till Christ
>Ope's the door.
>
>Prayer
>Is believing

In faith—
Nothing more![1]
—Gale Harris

[1] From THE FIRST BAPTIST CHURCH OF DALLAS by Leon McBeth. Copyright © 1968 by Zondervan Publishing House, Grand Rapids, Michigan. Used by permission.

54.

1. THE PROMISE: *"Give to every man that asketh of thee. . .Give, and it shall be given unto you; good measure, pressed down, and shaken together, and running over, shall men give into your bosom. For with the same measure that ye mete withal it shall be measured to you again"* (Luke 6:30,38).

2. THE POINT: The idea of *receiving* in the light of *giving* is usually associated in our thinking with what we give to God—an understanding, I hasten to add, which is certainly correct. However, as the context from the Sermon on the Mount quoted above shows, it is just as definitely true of giving to those in need.

3. THE PROOF: Before he left his homeland, England's famous pioneer missionary to China's interior, J. Hudson Taylor, worked for a physician for sixteen months at Hull, seeking medical and surgical skill for his Asian ministry. Although the good doctor had told him to remind him when his salary was due, Taylor determined, as part of the stern program he had established in endeavoring to learn to live by faith, he would not do so. He felt that failure at home, amidst familiar and friendly surroundings, would spell impossibility in the strange land of China.

On one occasion, when his quarterly salary was past due and he was down to a mere two shillings and sixpence (about 60 cents), a poverty-stricken man asked him to go and pray with his desperately ill wife. Upon arrival, he discovered a dying woman on a pallet in a squalid room, a three-day-old infant crying at her breast, plus another four or five half-starved children.

Taylor tried to pray but was unable, feeling to do so would be a mockery to God as long as he had money in his own pocket and refused to give it. He tried to speak words of comfort, but as long as he refused to trust God with an empty pocket, he felt like a hypocrite.

If his "fortune" had been in three coins—two shillings and one sixpence—he would have given part of it, but it was in the form of a half-crown and to offer anything would have meant giving it all. Finally, feeling the futility of trying to pray any longer, he arose from his knees only to hear the distraught father's anxious plea, "For God's sake, if you can help us, please do!"

Immediately the Lord's command, "Give to every man that asketh of thee," flashed through his mind, along with the statement of Solomon: "Where the word of a king is, there is power" (Ecclesiastes 8:4). Victory was instantaneous and, obeying the word of King Jesus, Taylor thrust his hand into his pocket and delivered his only coin to the needy husband. The dark, deserted streets of Hull resounded that night with the triumphant shouts of praise from the lips of a young man going home with empty pockets but a full heart.

Later, he wrote: "Not only was the poor woman's life saved, but my life, as I fully realized, had been saved too. It might have been a wreck—probably would have been as a Christian life—had not grace at that time conquered and the striving of God's Spirit been obeyed."

The sequel? On his knees before retiring, Taylor reminded his Saviour that unless the loan was a short one, he would have no dinner on the morrow. But with the morning came the mailman and a letter containing half a sovereign ($2.40), plus a pair of gloves! In describing it later, he exclaimed: "Four hundred per cent for twelve hours' investment!" God's bank, once again, had proven to be by far the best.

4. THE POEM:
>When nothing whereon to lean remains,
>When strongholds crumble to dust;
>When nothing is sure but that God still reigns,
>That is just the time to trust.
>
>'Tis better to walk by faith than sight,
>In this path of yours and mine;
>And the pitch-black night, when there's no other light,
>Is the time for our faith to shine.

55.

1. THE PROMISE: *"I beheld Satan as lightning fall from heaven. Behold, I give unto you power to tread on serpents and scorpions, and over all the power of the enemy: and nothing shall by any means hurt you"* (Luke 10:18,19).

2. THE POINT: Our adversary, the Devil, is a defeated foe. When the child of God is serving his Saviour, he may be assured that nothing can happen to him outside of the will of God. While Satan does have tremendous power, the servant of Jehovah has greater power. As a matter of fact, as Jesus pointed out, this includes power "OVER ALL THE POWER OF THE ENEMY."

3. THE PROOF: When John Gibson Paton was ministering for Christ in New Hebrides, one of the problems he faced was the hold the native "Sacred Men" had over the people, a combination of fear and awe that resulted in almost worship. These Sacred Men practiced a kind of sorcery or witchcraft which they called "Nahak." Strange as it may seem, these men were supposed to be able to bring about the death of any individual if they could but obtain even scraps of uneaten food the condemned one had left.

On one occasion, when Paton was trying to stop a war between two of the tribes—a rather common occupation for the poor missionary—three of the Sacred Men were present as he pleaded with the natives. As soon as his appeal was concluded, the Sacred Men arose and announced that they did not believe in the missionary's God nor did they need His help. They assured the cringing natives the Sacred Men were all-powerful in themselves and could give rain or drought, make war or peace, and cause the death, through Nahak, of *anyone*—whoever and whenever they pleased.

That was the opportunity for which the noble servant of God had long awaited!

Paton immediately turned to a lady standing nearby and requested some fruit from her basket. Eating a small portion, he turned to the Sacred Men and gave some of the remainder to each of the three, requesting that the people note what he had done. Then he challenged the Sacred Men to kill him, if they could, through their evil sorcery. The superstitious people were terrified at the missionary's challenge to the Sacred Men.

In a scene reminiscent of Elijah on Mount Carmel, Paton stood by and goaded the foolish trio as they went through their "pitiful mummery and foolish incantations." As his biographer later related: "It was a splendid chance for him to discredit them in the eyes of their dupes and victims, and he was anxious to make the most of it."

When nothing happened, the Sacred Men announced a gathering of all their group, giving assurance to the people that the missionary would be dead by the following Sunday. With the curse at "full strength," so to speak—through the combined efforts of all the Sacred Men—the people were sure that Paton's fate was sealed. As a matter of fact, little parties of sorrowing natives kept coming to the missionary's home the remainder of the week with fearful inquiries about his health. As the Lord's Day approached, their anxiety and fears increased to a fever pitch. They were certain it would be Paton's day of doom.

When Sunday arrived, Paton returned to the village where he had experienced the confrontation with the Sacred Men and the amazed natives could hardly believe their eyes when they beheld the smiling, healthy preacher. The Sacred Men were compelled to publicly acknowledge that their supposedly infallible Nahak was powerless to harm the missionary. And it was at this juncture that they made a fatal mistake: they used as an alibi that Paton was a Sacred Man like themselves and his God was more powerful than theirs!

Indeed, Paton assured them, his God was greater. Two of the three Sacred Men admitted their defeat and Paton's influence was greatly increased throughout every section of New Hebrides. He was able to move about without harm, even among the hostile tribes. As a matter of fact, he was even able to walk into the midst of their warring and they would stop hostilities while he pleaded with them to abandon the evils of war! On at least one occasion, they did.

4. THE POEM:

>Workman of God, oh, lose not heart,
>   But learn what God is like!
>And, in the darkest battlefield,
>   Thou shalt know where to strike.
>
>Oh, blest is he to whom is given
>   The instinct that can tell
>That God is on the field, when He
>   Is most invisible.

—Archbishop Frederick William Faber (1814-1863)

56.

1. THE PROMISE: *"Are not five sparrows sold for two farthings, and not one of them is forgotten before God? But even the very hairs of your head are all numbered. Fear not therefore: ye are of more value than many sparrows"* (Luke 12:6,7).

2. THE POINT: Almighty God, omnipotent Being that He is, takes careful note of the welfare of such tiny and insignificant (to

us) creatures as sparrows. Since this is true—and it is also true that He concerns Himself with an exact headcount of our hairs—there are no "little things" about our lives with which He is not vitally interested. He wants us to turn our most minute problems over to Him, seeking His involvement and assistance.

3. THE PROOF: When J. Hudson Taylor, noted missionary and founder of the China Inland Mission, was ministering in the United States, he spent considerable time with Dr. James H. Brookes in St. Louis. On one occasion he was scheduled to speak at a church in Southern Illinois on a Sunday. Dr. Brookes made all the arrangements for his trip and, on Saturday morning, took him down to the railroad station. Unhappily, just as they approached the station from one side, the train Mr. Taylor was to take to his destination was pulling out from the other side. If you have ever had the frustrating and exasperating experience of arriving at a departure point and seeing your transportation leaving, you can imagine how the gentlemen felt.

Actually, Dr. Brookes, since he was responsible for all the arrangements, felt worse than did Mr. Taylor. He immediately made inquiries and learned that no other train would depart for that city until night. However, in discussing the problem with the stationmaster, the latter pointed to another train in the yard and commented, "That train over there runs into Illinois and crosses another road down to where you want to go. They are supposed to make connections, but they never do."

Dr. Brookes went to check on other possibilities and when he returned he was startled to find Mr. Taylor standing on the rear platform of the train that "never" made the connection. He said, "Mr. Taylor, that won't work. It won't make the connection."

But Hudson Taylor simply smiled in his quiet way and said, "Goodbye, Doctor. My Father runs the trains!"

What happened? As the train pulled away from the depot, Mr. Taylor looked up the conductor and explained the importance of his engagement and his need for making the desired connection. The man expressed sympathy for the problem, but stated frankly he doubted very much that they would arrive in time, pointing out that they rarely did. Mr. Taylor returned to his seat and spent some time in quiet prayer, laying the problem before his Father.

When the train pulled into the station at the connecting point, the other train was standing there waiting. The conductor said, "Well, there it is. I really never thought we'd make it!" The missionary statesman had ample time to get off his train, cross the station, and board the other. As soon as he did, the train pulled out of the terminal and headed south.

The God who cares for sparrows had solved His servant's problem!

4. THE POEM:
> God understands the way you take,
>   He knows the trials of each day,
> And sympathizing, lends an ear
>   To hear you e'en before you pray.
> He walks with those who trust His love,
>   He holds them by the hand to guide;
> What need to fear or be dismayed,
>   With His dear Presence by your side!

57.

1. THE PROMISE: *"Consider the ravens: for they neither sow nor reap; which neither have storehouse nor barn; and God feedeth them: how much more are ye better than the fowls?"* (Luke 12:24).

2. THE POINT: The lowly raven—an "unclean" (Leviticus 11:13,15) fowl—is an object lesson to consider by weak Christians with timid faith. Since this bird—using none of the normal advantages of provision—is cared for by God and is well fed, how much more should the child of God expect to have his needs met by the Master!

3. THE PROOF: During the last century, a poor weaver lived in the little town of Wupperthal, Germany. While his material advantages were limited, his spiritual resources were abundant and all his neighbors knew him as a man who trusted the Lord for everything. Whenever trials, testings or perplexities came, he faced them with his favorite expression, "The Lord helps!" He meant it, too!

During one season of economic shortage, the mill where he worked ran short of orders and his employer told him he would have to let him go. When his earnest entreaties for reconsideration fell on deaf ears, he said, "Well, the Lord helps!" and returned home. When his wife met the news of his firing with loud weeping and wailing, he sought to comfort her with his usual assurance, "The Lord helps!"

Things went from bad to worse and eventually there was not a penny in the purse, a slice of bread in the pantry, or a stick of fuel in the fireplace. Even then, the weaver sought to keep up their courage by repeating, "The Lord helps!" A street boy heard the statement and, perhaps in saucy ridicule, picked a dead raven out of the street and tossed it into the house through an open window.

The pious saint picked up the dead bird, stroked its feathers compassionately, and said, "Poor creature! thou must have died of hunger." As he stroked, however, he felt something hard in its crop and decided to investigate. Cutting open the gullet, he found a shiny, gold necklace. Exclaiming, "The Lord helps," he rushed to the nearest goldsmith, who loaned him two dollars with which to buy food for his present need.

When he returned, the goldsmith had not only cleaned the necklace, but had identified the owner: the master of the mill who had fired the weaver! The saint immediately returned the trinket to its rightful owner, who, in turn, was ashamed and moved. It seems that he had accused a faithful servant of its theft and its return removed that breath of suspicion.

Remembering what the weaver had said when he dismissed him, the master thoughtfully declared, "Yes, the Lord helps; and now you not only go home richly rewarded, but I will no longer leave without work so pious a workman, whom the Lord so evidently stands by and helps; you shall henceforth be no more in need." Thus the One who fed Elijah through living ravens, fed and supplied the needs of the poor weaver through a dead one!

4. THE POEM:
>
> **The grasses are clothed**
> **And the ravens are fed**
> **from His store;**
> **But you, who are loved**
> **And guarded and led,**
> **How much more**
> **Will He clothe and feed you and give you His care?**
> **Then leave it with Him; He has everywhere**
> **Ample store.**

58. 1. THE PROMISE: *"But as many as received him, to them gave he power to become the sons of God, even to them that believe on his name"* (John 1:12).

2. THE POINT: Becoming a child of God is as simple as receiving Christ as Saviour. That receiving is explained as "believing on his name." When one puts his faith and trust in Jesus Christ, he is as ready for Heaven and as sure of Heaven as if he were already there.

3. THE PROOF: This promise, to the writer, is one of the sweetest in all the Bible even though it follows one of the most tragic statements of world literature ("He came unto his own, and his own received him not"). Why is it so precious? Because it was the promise I claimed when I first came to Christ, the one on which my own salvation is based.

As a young man of seventeen, out of high school for more than a year, I found myself at a Christian youth camp, the last place in the world I wanted to be. While the circumstances involved in that situation are too elaborate to relate now, suffice it to say that I was bombarded every morning in classes and every night in evangelistic services with the sharp, cutting, piercing Word of the Living God. Conviction deepened. Reformation was attempted and found to be utterly hopeless.

Finally, after several days which witnessed a steady stream of youthful personal workers approaching me to practice their skills, I agreed to talk to one of the leaders about the "problems" preventing my coming to Christ. My pastor's wife, Mrs. Reginald Matthews, took an open Bible and had me read the promise in John 1:12. Since I had said I would surrender to Christ if someone could show me what was "wrong" with certain worldly amusements and habits, I sought to debate those matters with her.

Again and again she simply returned to my basic need. When I would ask what was wrong with a certain thing, she would reply, "Bob, it says here that you need to *receive* Christ," or, "The Bible says you must *believe* in Him." After more than an hour of this consistent counseling, I came to the point of surrender.

Together we knelt on the sawdust floor of the humble, open-air tabernacle. My prayer was simple, short and most definitely to the point. I merely said, "Lord, if You'll have me, I'll have You," and, to the best of my ability, I received Jesus Christ as personal Saviour.

That did it! I am now saved, a child of God, ready for Heaven. *How do I know?* Because the One who "cannot lie" (Titus 1:2) guaranteed in writing, "As many as received him, to them gave he power to become the sons of God, even to them that believe on his name."

4. THE POEM:

    Naught have I gotten but what I received;
      Grace hath bestowed it since I have believed;
   Boasting excluded, pride I abase;
    I'm only a sinner saved by grace!

  Tears unavailing, no merit had I;

    Mercy had saved me, or else I must die;
    Sin had alarmed me, fearing God's face;
      But now I'm a sinner saved by grace!

Suffer a sinner whose heart overflows,
    Loving his Savior to tell what he knows;
Once more to tell it would I embrace—
    I'm only a sinner saved by grace.

Only a sinner saved by grace!
    Only a sinner saved by grace!
This is my story, to God be the glory,
    I'm only a sinner saved by grace!
                    —*James Martin Gray* (1851-1935)

59.

1. THE PROMISE: *". . .thou shalt see greater things than these"* (John 1:50).

2. THE POINT: While this promise was originally given to Nathanael after he had acclaimed Jesus as the Son of God and the King of Israel, it is indicative of every believer's walk in the life of faith. The more of the promises of God he appropriates, the greater the works of God in his life.

3. THE PROOF: When Louis Harms became pastor of the little Lutheran church in Hermansburg, Germany, about 1850, the whole area was in a sad state of spiritual lethargy and deadness. Under his dynamic leadership saints were revived, souls were saved and an impact with worldwide overtones resulted. Harms not only started a training school for missionaries, he built and maintained a mission ship and sent out and supported a vast number of missionaries in various parts of the world. He purchased a printing press and started publishing tracts, books and a monthly missionary magazine. He also established local reformatories.

This took huge sums of money. As a matter of fact, in 6 years his expenses totaled 115,676 crowns, an amount slightly more than this in American dollars. In the same period his receipts totaled 118,694 crowns, a fantastic income in those 19th century times.

He started with nothing. From whence came the money?

Harms prayed!

Telling of how the work was launched, he said: "I prayed fervently to the Lord, laid the matter in His hand, and as I rose up at midnight from my knees, I said in a voice that almost startled me in the quiet room, Forward now, in God's name! From that moment there never came a thought of doubt into my mind."

Some of his experiences in the victorious walk of faith are described in the following abridged extract from his own account: "It is wonderful, when one has nothing, and 10,000 crowns are laid in his hand by the dear Lord. I know from whom it all comes. I went to my God, and prayed diligently to Him, and received what I needed. To the question, Shall we print? we did not answer, Certainly we can; but we cried to the Lord, Grant it to us. And He granted it; for we immediately received 2,000 crowns, although the thought had not been known to anyone; we had only to take and be thankful.

"A short time ago I had to pay a merchant in behalf of the missions 550 crowns, and when the day was near I had only 400. Then I prayed to the Lord Jesus, that He would provide me with the deficiency. On the day before, three letters were brought; one from Schweim with 20, one from Bucksburg with 25, and one from Berlin with 100 crowns. The donors were anonymous. On the evening of the same day, a laborer brought me 10 crowns; so that I had not only enough, but five over.

I must tell you what brought tears into my eyes, and confirmed me anew in that word, 'Before they call, I will answer.' A medicine chest was urgently wanted for the mission. I reckoned up, to see if there was enough left to supply it. Before I had finished, and when I had not yet well begun to commend this matter to the Lord, a letter was brought in which the anonymous writer stated that for some time he had been collecting for the mission and had determined to purchase a medicine chest. The chest accompanied the letter; he only begged it might soon be sent out to the heathen."

Writing about 1857 and 1858, Harms enthused: "I needed for the mission 15,000 crowns, and the Lord gave me that, and 60 over. This year I needed double, and the Lord has given me double, and 140 over." He is truly the exceeding abundantly able God!

Are you letting Him do "greater things than these" for you?

4. THE POEM:

> There is an eye that never sleeps,
>   Beneath the wing of night;
> There is an ear that never shuts,
>   When sink the beams of light.
> There is an arm that never tires,
>   When human strength gives way;
> There is a love that never fails,
>   When earthly loves decay.
>
> That eye is fixed on seraph throngs;
> That ear is filled with angels' songs;
> That arm upholds the world on high;
> That love is throned beyond the sky.
>
> But there's a power which men can wield
>   When mortal aid is vain.
> That eye, that arm, that love to reach,
>   That listening ear to gain;
> That power is prayer, which soars on high,
> And feeds on bliss beyond the sky.
>
> —*Bishop Reginald Heber* (1783-1826)

60. 1. THE PROMISE: *"Jesus answered and said unto her, Whosoever drinketh of this water shall thirst again: But whosoever drinketh of the water that I shall give him shall never thirst; but the water that I shall give him shall be in him a well of water springing up into everlasting life"* (John 4:13,14).

2. THE POINT: No Christian need ever have an aching, empty heart. The provision for all of his heart's needs is included in the redemption his Saviour wrought at Calvary. Complete satisfaction is his for the taking—or the "drinking"!

3. THE PROOF: Early in 1870, one crushing blow after another fell upon that heroic pioneer missionary, J. Hudson Taylor. In February, his little son, Samuel, died. In March, he was forced to send his three oldest children to England. June saw the Tientsin massacre. In July, his dear wife and baby son, Noel, died within three days of each other. Shortly after that, Taylor was stricken with ague, dysentery and sleeplessness.

It was during those days that he learned the secret of John 4 in an experimental way for the first time. Although loving and appreciating it as a matter of ancient history in the past, now it was a thrilling personalized promise. Again and again—as often as twenty times a day—he returned to claim the promise. Never was he disappointed.

In describing it later, he wrote:

"What a promise! 'SHALL NEVER THIRST.' To *know* that 'shall' means shall; that 'never' means never; that 'thirst' means any unsatisfied need, may be one of the greatest revelations God ever made to our souls.

"Let us not, however, change the Saviour's words. Note carefully He does not say, Whosoever has drunk, but 'drinketh.' He speaks not of one draught, but of the continuous habit of the soul."

No wonder he was able to write to a friend: "No language can express what He has been and is to me. Never does He leave me; constantly does He cheer me with His love. He who once wept at the grave of Lazarus often now weeps in and with me. . .His own rest, His own peace, His own joy, He gives me. He kisses me with the kisses of His love, which are better than wine. Often I find myself wondering whether it is possible for her, who is taken, to have more joy in His presence than He has given me."

4. THE POEM:
>Thou, Lord, alone art all Thy children need,
>   And there is none beside;
>From Thee the streams of blessedness proceed,
>   In Thee the blest abide;
>Fountain of life and all-abounding grace,
>Our source, our center, and our dwelling place.

—Madame Jeanne Marie Bouvier de la Motte Guyon (1648-1717)

---

61. 1. THE PROMISE: *"Let not your heart be troubled: ye believe in God, believe also in me. In my Father's house are many mansions: if it were not so, I would have told you. I go to prepare a place for you. And if I go and prepare a place for you, I will come again, and receive you unto myself; that where I am, there ye may be also"* (John 14:1-3).

2. THE POINT: Here is one of the sweetest, most precious and oft-quoted promises in the Word of God. Our Lord, after affirming His equality with the Father and assuring His disciples that He is every bit as worthy of trust, outlines the eternal habitation for all who put their faith in Him. It is a blessed guarantee of Heaven, the greatest factor being that we will dwell with Him in a fellowship lasting forever.

3. THE PROOF: One of the great things about Heaven is that it can mean so many different things to a wide variety of people with greatly diversified needs—yet all of them be true. J. Wilbur

Chapman called attention to this, commenting:

" 'What do you think Heaven is?' asked Wilberforce, the Christian statesman, of Robert Hall, the Christian preacher. 'Well, Heaven is rest.' Ah, Robert Hall was a great sufferer. In the ruthless grip of an internal disease, writhing hours of the acutest agony were his daily lot. Rest, rest, for that poor, wracked, pained body of his, to him was Heaven.

"Said Wilberforce, 'I think of Heaven as love.' A happy home had he; a life large, generous and free from distress was his; the very image of bliss was his 'ain fireside,' and as he looked around it and caught the bright reflection of that cozy dancing fire on the gladsome looks of the dear home-loves, he naturally thought, 'why, Heaven is just "this present" transplanted, purified, glorified, and made eternal; love with the loving, my home!'

"It's true. There are many, many facets on that gem of the universe that catch, each a different ray of the sunlight of God, and each ray is beautiful and glad and healing to our blear and reek-filled eyes. There's the touch again of the 'vanished hand,' there's the sound again of the 'voice that is still.' There's the light-up again of the dear old faces that faded away in the chill gloom of the grave, there's life from the dead by yon crystal sea.

"Ay, but statesman and preacher alike were agreed with the apostle on the fact that the highest, the chief, the one crowning attraction of Heaven was 'to be with Christ.' "

4. THE POEM:

>Some day the silver cord will break,
> And I no more as now shall sing;
>But, oh, the joy when I shall wake
> Within the palace of the King!
>
>Some day my earthly house will fall,
> I cannot tell how soon 'twill be;
>But this I know—my All in All
> Has now a place in Heav'n for me.
>
>Some day, when fades the golden sun
> Beneath the rosy-tinted west,
>My blessed Lord will say, "Well done!"
> And I shall enter into rest.

Some day: till then I'll watch and wait,
My lamp all trimmed and burning bright,
That when my Saviour opes the gate,
My soul to Him may take its flight.
—*Fanny J. Crosby* (1820-1915)

62. 1. THE PROMISE: *"And whatsoever ye shall ask in my name, that will I do, that the Father may be glorified in the Son. If ye shall ask any thing in my name, I will do it"* (John 14:13,14).

2. THE POINT: Our Saviour is anxious to answer the believer's every prayer and thereby bring glory to the Heavenly Father. So much is this so, He emphasized to His disciples that ANY THING they wanted should be a subject for prayer and WHATSOEVER they asked in His name would be given. Obviously, He intended the smallest problems to be matters of serious prayer.

3. THE PROOF: Before Dr. Henry Clay Trumbull (1830-1903) became editor of *The Sunday School Times,* while still making his home in Connecticut, he was rushing to catch a midnight train for Boston. While he was folding a manuscript which had to be placed into the mail for a Chicago magazine, *The National Teacher,* he suddenly was startled by a cry of pain from his wife on the floor above him.

Racing upstairs, he discovered that she had burned herself on a lamp. Since the burn was slight, he returned to his study to finish preparing the manuscript for mailing. To his utter dismay, it was no where to be found! Frantically and fruitlessly he searched the desk, the floor, the hall, the stairs, the rooms above and the eight or ten pockets of his clothing. Since neither the midnight train nor the editorial deadline could wait, he was desperate to find the missing manuscript immediately. Down on his knees he went, earnestly beseeching his Heavenly Father for help. Quickly came the clear impression: Stand up, and throw off your coat and vest.

When he did so, there in an inner vest pocket—which he did not even know he had—was the lost manuscript. Late as was the hour, he took time to drop to his knees again and warmly thank his Father for His goodness, then he rushed to the railroad depot, mailing the papers as he went.

Later, when recounting the incident, he wrote: "For although this was all within the realm of the natural, I was nonetheless helpless to find the missing paper within the time allowed me; and I needed God's supernatural oversight of the natural in order to enable me to do my duty for Him in my little sphere. And He came to my relief with His guiding voice, as He is ever ready to do for His children, according to their need and faith."

4. THE POEM:

What a Friend we have in Jesus, All our sins and griefs to bear!
What a privilege to carry EV'RYTHING to God in prayer!
O what peace we often forfeit, O what needless pain we bear,
All because we do not carry EV'RYTHING to God in prayer!

Have we trials and temptations? Is there trouble anywhere?
We should never be discouraged, Take it to the Lord in prayer.
Can we find a friend so faithful Who will all our sorrows share?
Jesus knows our ev'ry weakness, Take it to the Lord in prayer.

—*Joseph Scriven* (1819-1886)

---

63. 1. THE PROMISE: *"If ye abide in me, and my words abide in you, ye shall ask what ye will, and it shall be done unto you"* (John 15:7).

2. THE POINT: Unlimited power in prayer is available to the one who abides in Christ, with His words abiding in him. The idea of abiding, as S. D. Gordon points out, "does

not mean to hire a night's lodging. It does not mean a lumberman's shack, nor a miner's shanty. By contrast it means moving into a brownstone house to stay, with the title deed in your own name." That kind of abiding gets prayer results far beyond human comprehension!

3. THE PROOF: One area in which this prayer power is manifested relates to the conversion of cases considered impossible by some. The noted 19th century evangelist, Charles G. Finney, in his lecture, "The Spirit of Prayer," recounts the following:

"I was acquainted with an individual who used to keep a list of persons that he was especially concerned for, and I have had the opportunity to know a multitude of persons for whom he became thus interested, who were immediately converted. I have seen him pray for persons on his list when he was literally in agony for them; and have sometimes known him to call on some other person to help him pray for such-a-one. I have known his mind to fasten thus on an individual of hardened, abandoned character, and who could not be reached in any ordinary way.

"In a town in a north part of the state of New York, where there was a revival, there was a certain individual who was a most violent and outrageous opposer. He kept a tavern, and used to delight in swearing, at a desperate rate, whenever there were Christians within hearing, on purpose to hurt their feelings. He was so bad that one man said he believed he should have to sell his place, or give it away, and move out of town, for he could not live near a man that swore so.

"This good man, that I was speaking of, was passing through the town, and heard of the case, and was very much grieved and distressed for the individual. He took him on his praying list. The case weighed on his mind, when he was asleep and when he was awake. He kept thinking about him, and praying for him, for days. And the first we knew of it, this ungodly man came into a meeting, and got up and confessed his sins, and poured out his soul. His barroom immediately became the place where they held prayer meetings."

4. THE POEM:
>
> There is a place where thou canst touch the eyes
> Of blinded men to instant, perfect sight;
> There is a place where thou canst say "Arise!"
> To dying captives bound in chains of night;
> There is a place where Heaven's resistless power
> Responsive moves to thine insistent plea;
> There is a place—a silent, trusting hour—
> Where God Himself descends and fights for thee.
> Where is that blessed place—dost thou ask "Where?"
> O Soul, it is the secret place of prayer.
>
> —*Adelaide Addison Pollard* (1862-1934)

64.

1. THE PROMISE: *"And we know that all things work together for good to them that love God, to them who are the called according to his purpose"* (Romans 8:28).

2. THE POINT: God has a plan for each believer's life and, in the long run, everything that happens to the believer ultimately is for his advantage. Sorrow and joy, good and bad, disappointments and thrills all "work together" to make a finished product which benefits the believer.

3. THE PROOF: Years ago, a shipwrecked man managed to make it to a small uninhabited island. There he built a small shelter which offered protection from the elements and the wild animals. Praying continuously for rescue, he nonetheless labored to build up a small store of supplies for survival.

However, returning home one afternoon from a foraging trip and climbing the hill which looked down upon his residence, he was startled and chagrined to see his meager possessions going up in flames. *Gone* were his supplies, *wasted* was all the time and effort he had put into building the shelter, *in vain* was everything he had accomplished since arriving on the island.

His heart sank within him as he moaned, "Lord, why did You have to let this happen? This is tragedy upon tragedy. First, the shipwreck; *now this!*"

A few hours later, as he tried to sift through the smoldering wreckage to salvage some of his labors, he looked up to see a vessel approaching the harbor. Excitedly, he ran to the shore and greeted the men who were rowing toward land in a small boat from the ship.

When they got within hailing distance, one of the men cried: "Hello! Do you need help?"

Assuring them that he most certainly did, they replied: "We thought so when we saw your distress signal!" What he thought to be tragedy was triumph! The burning of his feeble belongings was seen by the sailors and interpreted as a signal of distress. Oh, how many times our "burnings" are, in actuality, God's signals of deliverance!

4. THE POEM:

>**Is the road very dreary?**
>>**Patience yet!**
>
>**Rest will be sweeter if thou art a-weary,**
>**And after night cometh the morning cheery—**
>>**Just bide a wee and dinna fret!**
>
>**The clouds have silver lining,**
>>**Don't forget!**
>
>**And though He's hidden, still the sun is shining,**
>**Courage instead of tears and vain repining,**
>>**Just bide a wee and dinna fret!**

65. 1. THE PROMISE: *"Dearly beloved, avenge not yourselves, but rather give place unto wrath: for it is written, Vengeance is mine; I will repay, saith the Lord"* (Romans 12:19).

2. THE POINT: No matter how strong the temptation or how great the provocation, the child of God is never to take vengeance into his own hands. When we commit the matter of "wrongs" into the hands of our Lord, He is abundantly able to turn them into "rights" in a way bringing glory to Himself and blessing to the saint.

3. THE PROOF: An interesting incident took place in the life of that noble Hebrew Christian, David Baron. It seems that a Dutch lady who loved the Lord and was burdened about Hebrew evangelism had promised Mr. Baron she would leave the mission 10,000 gulden in her will. After her Home-going, her attorney wrote Baron saying he was aware his client wanted the mission to have that amount, but that the legacy was being disputed by the woman's relatives. He requested permission to represent the mission in court in an effort to obtain the money.

Mr. Baron immediately replied: "We never go to earthly courts in such matters, but we will present our case before the court in Heaven and trust God to give us a righteous judgment."

There was a delay of about two years while certain relatives were traced, but the attorney finally wrote again to say that all had been found and again he requested authority to represent the mission in claiming the 10,000 gulden. The answer once more was a firm refusal, stating again that the matter was being presented before the court of Heaven.

Some additional weeks passed and word came again from the lawyer. He wrote that the matter, much to his surprise, had been settled amicably. The woman's relatives had decided to accept half of the estate and give the mission the other half. This turned out to be approximately 20,000 gulden, *an amount double what the woman had bequeathed!* Not bad interest for waiting two years before Heaven's court! Well did the attorney comment that he could now understand why Mr. Baron preferred to take his case to Heaven's court.

The money was enclosed in the lawyer's letter, arriving shortly before Mr. Baron himself was called to Heaven and proving to be a real Godsend in the years of testing for the mission which followed his death.

4. THE POEM:
> Why fret thee, soul,
> For things beyond thy small control?
> But do thy part, and thou shalt see
> Heaven will take charge of them and thee.
> Sow then thy seed, and wait in peace
> The Lord's increase.

66. 1. THE PROMISE: *"For none of us liveth to himself, and no man dieth to himself"* (Romans 14:7).

2. THE POINT: Everyone has tremendous influence on others. While wrong actions obviously influence others for evil, just as certainly good actions and right behavior influence others for obedience to the will of God.

3. THE PROOF: George Muller was one of Christendom's choicest saints and believers today are still marveling over his 19th century feats of faith. Yet the mighty miracles he wrought for Christ and the church might never have been accomplished had it not been for another who willing paid a price in service.

In 1826, through reading missionary papers, Muller yielded himself for Christian service. However, an attachment for a young lady caused him to remove his eyes from his goal, choking his spirit and making his prayer life formal and cold. In fact, he eventually reached the place where he almost never prayed. During this time of spiritual barrenness he became acquainted with Herman Ball, a youth from the home of immense wealth who had relinquished all his comforts in order to reach the Jews of Poland.

Muller said: "His example made a deep impression on me. I was led to apply his case to my own, and to compare myself with him, for I had given up the work of the Lord, and I may say the Lord Himself, for the sake of a girl. The result of this comparison was that I was enabled to give up the connection which I had entered upon without prayer, and which thus had led me away from the Lord. When I was enabled to be decided, the Lord smiled on me, and I was, for the first time in my life, able fully and unreservedly to give up myself to Him."

Thus a ministry was spared and the world immensely benefited by Muller's life and labors, all because of the godly influence of a youth who determined to put God first in his life.

4. THE POEM:

>What wouldst thou be?
>A blessing to each one surrounding me;
>A chalice of dew to the weary heart,
>A sunbeam of joy bidding sorrow depart,
>To the storm tossed vessel a beacon light,
>A nightingale song in the darkest night,
>A beckoning hand to a far-off goal,
>An angel of love to each friendless soul,
>Such would I be.
>Oh, that SUCH happiness were for me.
>
>*—Frances Ridley Havergal* (1836-1879)

67.

1. THE PROMISE: *"Now we have received, not the spirit of the world, but the spirit which is of God; that we might know the things that are freely given to us of God. Which things also we speak, not in the words which man's wisdom teacheth, but which the Holy Ghost teacheth; comparing spiritual things with spiritual. . .But he that is spiritual judgeth all things, yet he himself is judged of no man. For who hath known the mind of the Lord, that he may instruct him? But we have the mind of Christ"* (I Corinthians 2:12,13,15,16).

2. THE POINT: The Bible is a spiritual Book, given by the Spirit of God in its very words. Since this is true, the Spirit of God is fully able to teach its spiritual truths to those who depend upon Him to do so, seeking His mind to be revealed.

3. THE PROOF: When the noted British Bible teacher, G. Campbell Morgan, was in the days of his early ministry, the swift rise of materialistic and rationalistic philosophy, with its sneers at the Word of God, was blitzing both England and America. Colonel Bob Ingersoll was leading the attack in the States and Charles Bradlaugh was the driving force of the movement in England. The assault was so strong that many churches were abandoning former theological positions and charges and countercharges were sweeping the literary world.

Young Morgan was caught in the whirlpool and questions about God and the Bible began to trouble him deeply. He purchased and read the "Is God Knowable?" books flooding the market at that time, almost all of which concluded He was not. Other books followed, in defense of the historic Christian position, but, strangely, they only served to confuse him more. Later in life he described this experience as like "passing through a trackless desert," and eventually he came to the place where he was no longer sure that the Bible was indeed God's authoritative, infallible Word to man.

Morgan cancelled every preaching engagement on his schedule. Then he gathered all the books he had been studying on the subject, both pro and con, taking them to a corner cupboard, putting them inside, closing the door and turning the key in the lock. Telling of the experience in later years, he would say, "I can hear the click of that lock now!"

After locking the books in the cupboard, he went to a bookshop and purchased a new Bible. When he arrived home, he went to his room, commenting to himself: "I am no longer sure that this is what my father claims it to be—the Word of God. But of this I AM sure. If it BE the Word of God, and if I come to it with my unprejudiced and open mind, it will bring assurance to my soul of itself." And shut up alone with God in his room, with the Holy

Spirit being His only instructor, the Divine Revelator led him into *positive* assurance that the Bible *is* all it claims to be: the verbally inspired, infallible Word of Almighty God!

Describing his experience 55 years later, Morgan said: "That Bible *found* me. I began to read and study it then, in 1883. I have been a student ever since, and I still am." He went on, as church history shows, to become one of the greatest expositors of the Word of God in the 19th and 20th centuries.

The Bible, taught by its Author, the Holy Spirit, is still its own best defense!

4. THE POEM:

> There are some who believe the Bible,
> And some who believe a part,
> Some who trust with a reservation,
> And some with all their heart.
> But I know that its ev'ry promise
> Is firm and true always,
> It is tried as the precious silver,
> And it means just what it says.
>
> It assures me of salvation,
> Thro' Jesus' precious blood,
> For the souls that trust His mercy,
> And yield themselves to God.
> And I claim for myself the promise,
> And just begin to praise,
> For it says I am saved by trusting,
> And I trust just as it says.
>
> It is strange we trust each other,
> And only doubt our Lord;
> We will take the word of mortals
> And yet distrust His Word;
> But, oh, what light and glory,
> Would shine o'er all our days,
> If we always would remember
> That He means just what He says.
>
> —*Albert B. Simpson* (1843-1919)

68.

1. THE PROMISE: *"There hath no temptation taken you but such as is common to man: but God is faithful, who will not suffer you to be tempted above that ye are able; but will with the temptation also make a way to escape, that ye may be able to bear it"* (I Corinthians 10:13).

2. THE POINT: Every man faces temptations. No temptation is unique. But every Christian may be assured, on the basis of God's matchless faithfulness and mercy, that he will never, NEVER face a temptation over which he cannot triumph. Furthermore, God never allows a temptation but what He makes victory possible for the tempted.

3. THE PROOF: During the nineteenth century, the chaplain of a Prussian regiment was a man by the name of LaFontaine. During his services one Lord's Day he preached a strong sermon on the wickedness of a hasty temper. In his congregation was a major who had quite a reputation for "flying off the handle" at the slightest provocation.

The next day the major confronted the chaplain and accused him of "going beyond his liberty." While frankly acknowledging that he had thought of him while preaching, LaFontaine assured the officer that he had no intention whatsoever of being personal. He insisted he had simply been delivering the message God had laid upon his heart for that hour. The major left, but not until he said repeatedly, "It is no use! I have a hasty temper and I cannot control it. It is impossible!"

The very next Sunday, Chaplain LaFontaine preached a message on the theme of self-deception. Dealing with the excuses men make, he said: "Why, a man will declare that it is impossible for him to control his temper, when he very well knows that, were the same provocation to happen in the presence of his sovereign, he not only could but would control himself entirely. And yet he dares to say that the continual presence of the King of kings imposes upon him neither restraint nor fear."

The next day, just as with the previous week, the major was

back to confront the clergyman. This time, however, it was to humbly acknowledge: "You were right yesterday, chaplain. Hereafter, when you see me in danger of falling, remind me of the King's presence."

4. THE POEM:

> I cannot do it alone;
>   The waves run fast and high,
> And the fogs close all around,
>   The light goes out in the sky;
> But I know that we two
>   Shall win in the end,
>   Jesus and I.
>
> I could not guide it myself,
>   My boat on life's wild sea;
> There's One who sits by my side,
>   Who pulls and steers with me.
> And I know that we two
>   Shall safe enter port,
>   Jesus and I.

69. 1. THE PROMISE: *"Blessed be God, even the Father of our Lord Jesus Christ, the Father of mercies, and the God of all comfort; Who comforteth us in all our tribulation, that we may be able to comfort them which are in any trouble, by the comfort wherewith we ourselves are comforted of God"* (II Corinthians 1:3,4).

2. THE POINT: Trials and tribulations are instructive! The individual who, in the midst of sorrow and anguish, turns to the Heavenly Father for comfort will be rewarded with a caliber of mercy not only sufficient for the need, but ample for sharing triumphantly with others who are passing through deep waters.

3. THE PROOF: Dr. George W. Truett, whose own ministry

was enhanced in effectiveness through a personal sorrow he carried most of his life, told of two young mothers in his acquaintance.

The first had a beautiful baby who died after a brief illness. Neither she nor her husband knew Christ in His saving power. As a matter of fact, both parents were extremely worldly and Truett had a difficult time reaching them. But the minister's kindness to them during their sorrow, his remarks at the funeral, his presence with them to and from the cemetery—all added to make them receptive to his invitation to church. After only a few Sundays, both were happily saved.

Some months later, Dr. Truett was summoned by another mother to conduct the funeral of her sweet, flaxen-haired little girl. Like the first mother, she was not a Christian and she seemed inconsolable in her grief. Nothing Truett said, no Scripture he read, no word he offered seemed to help. Then, as a quartet sang, the first mother stepped up to her, placed her arm about her, and softly whispered: "Jennie, dear, it is going to be all right!"

"Oh, Mary," responded the grieving one, "how can it be all right? Everything about it is bad and dark and wrong. It cannot be all right!"

Then the first mother said: "I passed through the same experience. I know what you are passing through. Through my experience God called me to Himself and, in the darkness, I came to Him. His comfort was more than sufficient. Jennie, dear, He will comfort you, too, if you will let Him. He is calling you to Himself. If you will trust in Him, He will bring you out."

And Truett said: "The first mother did more for the second mother than I could have done, maybe in days and months, for the first little mother had traveled that road of suffering herself!"

4. THE POEM:
>I walked a mile with Pleasure,
>She chattered all the way,
>But left me none the wiser,

For all she had to say.

I walked a mile with Sorrow,
And not a word said she;
But, oh, the things I learned from her,
When Sorrow walked with me!

—*Robert B. Hamilton*

70. 1. THE PROMISE: *"Therefore if any man be in Christ, he is a new creature: old things are passed away; behold, all things are become new"* (II Corinthians 5:17).

2. THE POINT: Jesus Christ, immediately and completely, not only forgives the sinner of his vile transgressions, but He also completely changes the life and nature of that individual. So striking and remarkable is this spiritual revolution that the Word of God fittingly describes it as becoming a new creation!

3. THE PROOF: In reading the remarkable volume, *Jerry McAuley and His Mission,* by Arthur Bonner, we were impressed again and again with God's power, not only to save, but to transform. One of the trophies of God's redeeming grace the book described was "Rowdy" Brown. Bonner wrote:

"He was a mate on the Liverpool packets and a savage. He hated religion. He once saw a man sitting in the fo'c'sle of a ship reading the Bible. Without a word, Brown kicked the man in the mouth, knocking his teeth out, and permanently disfiguring his face. He was afraid of no one. He once stood boldly and cursed a man who had two pistols in his hands. The man fired both guns. Brown was hit but survived.

"He was living at Rhode's New Sailors' Home on Pearl Street when he heard that a chum had been converted at Jerry's. He grabbed a bottle of whisky and started toward the mission. He swore that if his mate got up to testify he would tear his mouth open and pour the whisky down his throat.

"The meeting began and Brown sat holding his black bottle, waiting for his shipmate to stand up. He listened intently to be ready to act. He felt himself tremble. They were telling stories and describing feelings that could have been his own. When his chum testified Brown just sat and listened. When prayers were invited at the end of the meeting Rowdy Brown stood up and called out, 'Oh, pray for me.'

"Everyone knew him. McAuley and others gathered around and Brown moaned and seemed to be torn with anguish. He became calm and went home. He returned the following night and still did not feel converted. But he went home and prayed and as he got into his bed he suddenly felt the thrill of conversion. He jumped out of bed again and shouted praises of God so loudly he awakened his roommate, who thought he was drunk.

"Rowdy Brown became as rough and ready in his new life as he had been in his old. He would sometimes grab a sailor on the street and drag him into the meeting. When the invitation was given for prayers he would go over to someone he believed should be saved and hoist him up to his feet. He would come back from a voyage and give a sizable part of his earnings to the mission.

"He even started his own rescue mission at sea. There is a story told of him aboard the West India brig *Nellie,* in the harbor of Matanzas, Cuba. He stretched a big canvas on the deck as an awning and had a sign painted: JERRY McAULEY'S PRAYER MEETING HERE THIS AFTERNOON AT THREE O'CLOCK. He sent boats out to collect sailors from other ships and touched off a small revival in the port."[1]

Such is the dynamic power of the Gospel to change lives.

4. THE POEM:

Lord Jesus, I long to be perfectly whole;
  I want Thee forever to live in my soul;
Break down ev'ry idol, cast out ev'ry foe;
  Now wash me and I shall be whiter than snow.

Lord Jesus, for this I most humbly entreat;

I wait, blessed Lord, at Thy crucified feet.
By faith, for my cleansing I see Thy blood flow—
Now wash me and I shall be whiter than snow.

Lord Jesus, Thou seest I patiently wait;
Come now, and within me a new heart create;
To those who have sought Thee, Thou never saids't no,
Now wash me and I shall be whiter than snow.

—*James Nicholson* (1828-1896)

Copyright©1967 by Loizeaux Brothers, Inc., Neptune, New Jersey. Used by permission.

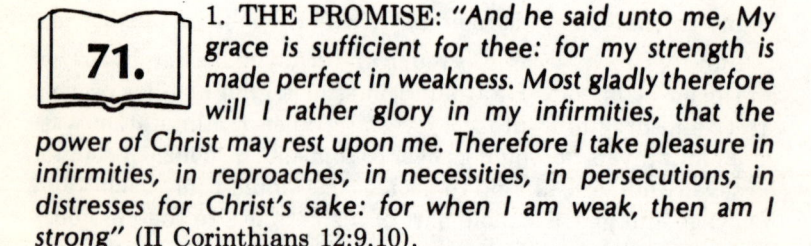

71.

1. THE PROMISE: *"And he said unto me, My grace is sufficient for thee: for my strength is made perfect in weakness. Most gladly therefore will I rather glory in my infirmities, that the power of Christ may rest upon me. Therefore I take pleasure in infirmities, in reproaches, in necessities, in persecutions, in distresses for Christ's sake: for when I am weak, then am I strong"* (II Corinthians 12:9,10).

2. THE POINT: Weakness is not necessarily a curse; often it is a blessing without which God's strength and power would not and could not be realized. Physical infirmities have time and again been the medium through which a believer exchanged God's "good" in his life for God's "best," as in the case of the Apostle Paul.

3. THE PROOF: It was a bleak, sultry afternoon in 1929. Paul Hutchens, a highly promising young evangelist who was soon to begin a great united evangelistic crusade in a Colorado city, had parked his automobile alongside a quiet country road a few miles out of Santa Rosa, California. Any appearance of despondency on the preacher's part could be explained from the fact that his

physician had just informed him of an advanced case of tuberculosis.

From a broken heart he sobbed to God: "Oh, my Father! I plead with Thee! Hear my prayer now! NOW! I ask Thee; yea, I expect Thee to heal me. This moment! Souls are dying without Christ! Please God! For Jesus' sake!" Yet even as he wept and prayed, he was conscious of the seemingly cruel answer which echoed in his heart: "No, No, NO!" It was a terribly discouraged, defeated, despairing preacher who finally drove back to town.

Yet less than 15 years later—as far back as 1943—the same preacher took pen in hand to declare, in his book, *When God Says "NO"*: "In 1929 my parish was local, wherever I chanced to be. Today it is the world. Not hundreds of people; not thousands, nor yet hundreds of thousands. But millions! More than 200,000 copies of my stories are now in circulation throughout the world—stories which would never have been written had the answer to my prayer been 'Yes.' For it has been by battle with tuberculosis that I have discovered and developed the talent for writing. Many of my published novels have been broadcast serially over one of America's large radio stations, reaching potentially millions. Thousands of letters have come telling of blessings received, of Christians being strengthened, of young people surrendering their lives to Christ.

"My own life is rich and full. While it is true, my health is now greatly improved, it has been at the cost of ten years of semi-invalidism, suffering, a total of three-and-one-half years in bed and a number of operations—one of them a triple major operation involving the removal of a number of ribs and the permanent collapse of one lung.

"The fruit of that cost is a mind enriched by voluminous reading, prayer and fellowship and deeper appreciation of God's presence in times of testing, a deeper love for my family and a world-wide parish; yes, and the continuous satisfaction of knowing that many are coming to Jesus Christ, through whom alone they can be saved."[1]

And, remember, Hutchens wrote that testimonial over a quarter of a century ago!

4. THE POEM:

The vine demands strong purging if fruit is to be seen;
  The Husbandman is urging that branches be kept clean.
He to the wall may pin us, the vine may oft be fled;
  "God will kill nothing in us that is not better dead."

Have courage then, my brother, though sharp may be the knife;
  The flesh may shrink and quiver, and thou despair of life.
God is at work within thee, He will lift up thy head;
  "God will kill nothing in thee that is not better dead."[1]

[1] From WHEN GOD SAYS "NO" AND OTHER RADIO ADDRESSES by Paul Hutchens. Copyright, 1943, by Wm. B. Eerdmans Publishing Co., Grand Rapids, Michigan. Used by permission.

72.

1. THE PROMISE: *"He that soweth to his flesh shall of the flesh reap corruption; but he that soweth to the Spirit shall of the Spirit reap life everlasting. And let us not be weary in well doing: for in due season we shall reap, if we faint not"* (Galatians 6:8,9).

2. THE POINT: Just as sinful sowing brings tragic reaping, so sowing directed by the Holy Spirit produces blessed results, even though it may not appear so at the time. And saints led by the Spirit of God in witnessing should never give up! Reaping eventually follows faithfulness just as surely as morning's brightness eventually follows midnight's utter blackness.

3. THE PROOF: In my biography of Dr. John R. Rice, *Man Sent from God,* I related the conversion experience of his father as follows: It was in Gainesville as a young man of about thirty that Will, as his friends affectionately called him, attended a few services of a local revival meeting. To his acute embarrassment, a cowboy companion slipped up during the invitation one night,

threw an arm around his shoulder and softly whispered, "Will, I'm praying for you. I am anxious about your soul. God has saved me and I would like you to take my Saviour, too."

The cowboy drew himself haughtily erect and sharply responded, "I'm a grown man and I know what I want to do without anyone telling me. I came to enjoy the sermon but if I have to be disturbed and embarrassed by people coming to me publicly, urging me to become a Christian when I am not ready, then I will not come to the meeting any more. If anyone talks to me again, I will never come back."

The Christian friend left, resolving not to disturb him again; but a few nights later the urging of the Holy Spirit was so strong in his heart that he approached the lost cowboy the second time, saying, "Will, I didn't intend to come back, but something compels me. I am so burdened about you. I cannot get any peace and I am so anxious for you to be saved."

Will threw down his song book, grabbed his big Stetson hat, angrily turned to his friend and said as he stomped out, "I told you that if you did not leave me alone I would never darken the door of this church again as long as I live! Perhaps it will give you some pleasure to remember that you have driven me from the house of God!"

At the time, Will was rooming with his brother and sister-in-law. Arriving home before the others, he went directly to his room and retired for the night, but could not sleep. For hours he tossed upon his bed without relief. He would get up, smoke, pace back and forth across the room, then return to his bed, but slumber simply would not come. The long hours of restlessness were accompanied by increasing, deep conviction of sin. Eventually he said to himself, "What a fool I am! The best friend I have in the world came to me because he loved me, wanted to see me saved and keep me out of Hell, and I, like an ill-bred wretch, insulted him and drove him away. Now no one else will speak to me and it will only serve me right if I end up in Hell!"

Finally, at four o'clock in the morning, he fell on his knees beside his bed, confessed his sins, and cried out to God for mercy and salvation. Sweet peace instantly came into his heart and he found the rest he sought in Jesus Christ. When the janitor arrived at the church the next morning at five o'clock to open the doors for the sunrise prayer service, he found Will Rice, the man who had vowed only the night before he would never return, sitting on the front steps waiting for the others to come so he could tell them what had happened!

Shortly thereafter Will felt called to preach.[1]

4. THE POEM:

ISAIAH 49:2

The bow is bent,
The shaft is sent
And God has aimed it well,
Though it may be
We cannot see
The mark where it shall dwell,
We'll someday find
The Marksman's mind
Determined where it went.
Though short the shot,
The happy lot:
The polished shaft is spent.[2]

—*Bill Harvey*

[1] From MAN SENT FROM GOD by Robert L. Sumner. Copyright 1959, Sword of the Lord Publishers, owner. Used by permission.

[2] From 100 BILL HARVEY POEMS. Copyright 1974 by Sword of the Lord Publisher, Murfreesboro, Tennessee. Used by permission.

73. 1. THE PROMISE: *"The eyes of your understanding being enlightened; that ye may know what is the hope of his calling, and what the riches of the glory of his inheritance in the saints"* (Ephesians 1:18).

2. THE POINT: The hope of His calling is a calling both to sonship and to service. The riches of His glory is literally "the glorious wealth of His inheritance" and our share of that wealth is so great it will take Him "the ages to come" to show us (Ephesians 2:7).

3. THE PROOF: The late Charles E. Fuller, so widely used on the "Old-Fashioned Revival Hour" broadcast, gave this testimony:

"Though brought up in a Christian home, my main desire on graduation from college was to get married and get rich. During the next seven years I did get married and became very successful in business—becoming the manager of an orange packing house in Southern California.

"But then one day I read that Paul Rader would be speaking in Los Angeles the next Sunday and, knowing that he used to be an athlete like myself, I decided to go to hear him. He preached on Ephesians 1:18, a message on Heaven—dealing with 'the riches of the glory of his inheritance in the saints'—and as he spoke on what Heaven would be like, and what one would have to be like in order to be admitted to Heaven, I realized that I was not fit for Heaven.

"I did not raise my hand when the invitation was given; instead I left the church and got into my old Franklin car and drove to a park in Hollywood. There I parked the car under some eucalyptus trees and cried to God, saying, 'O God, if there is a God, save me now.' And God saved me then.

"He also enabled me to see that there was a plan for my life. Ephesians 2:10 meant a great deal to me. 'For we are his workmanship, created in Christ Jesus unto good works, which God hath before ordained that we should walk in them.' I had confidence, as a result of this verse, that God had my future all mapped out. Two years later I left the packing house and began to train for the gospel ministry."

4. THE POEM:
My Father is rich in houses and lands,

> He holdeth the wealth of the world in His hands!
> Of rubies and diamonds, of silver and gold,
> > His coffers are full—He has riches untold.
>
> I once was an outcast stranger on earth,
> > A sinner by choice and an alien by birth;
> But I've been adopted, my name's written down—
> > An heir to a mansion, a robe, and a crown.
>
> A tent or a cottage, why should I care?
> They're building a palace for me over there!
> Tho' exiled from home, yet still I may sing:
> > All glory to God, I'm a child of the King!
>
> —*Harriett Eugenia Peck Buell* (1834-1910)

74.

1. THE PROMISE: *"For to me to live is Christ, and to die is gain. . .having a desire to depart, and to be with Christ; which is far better"* (Philippians 1:21,23).

2. THE POINT: The moment a child of God dies he is with Christ. There is no soul sleep, no purgatory, no intermediary state of any kind. "Absent from the body. . .present with the Lord" (II Corinthians 5:8). Fear is thus banished from death for the Christian.

3. THE PROOF: Dr. Samuel Rutherford, noted theologian and professor of divinity at the University of St. Andrews, was one of Scotland's greatest lights. Because of his stirring defense of liberty and religion, the Parliament of Scotland summoned him for trial.

When the call came, Rutherford was on his deathbed. He told the messenger, "Tell the Parliament that I have received a summons to a higher bar. I must needs answer that first; and when the day you name shall come, I shall be where few of you shall enter."

As death's darkness began to settle upon him, he turned to the ministers gathered around his bedside and said, "There is none like Christ. Oh, dear brethren, pray for Christ, preach Christ, do all for Christ. Feed the flock of God. And, oh, beware of men-pleasing!"

Then, recovering from a fainting spell, he exclaimed: "I feel, I feel, I believe, I joy, I rejoice, I feed on manna. My eyes shall see my Redeemer and I shall be ever with Him. And what would you more? I have been a sinful man, but I stand at the best pass that ever a man did. Christ is mine and I am His. Glory, glory to my Creator and Redeemer forever! Glory shines in Immanuel's land. Oh, for arms to embrace Him! Oh, for a well-tuned harp!" Thus he continued exulting in God his Saviour to the last as one in the full vision of joy and glory.

4. THE POEM:

> Oh, what is life?
> A toil, a strife,
> Were it not lighted by Thy love divine.
> I ask not wealth,
> I crave not health:
> Living or dying, Lord, I would be Thine!
>
> Oh, what is death,
> When the poor breath
> In parting can the soul to Thee resign!
> While patient love
> Her trust doth prove,
> Living or dying, Lord, I would be Thine!
>
> Throughout my days,
> Be constant praise
> Uplift to Thee from out this heart of mine;
> So shall I be
> Brought nearer Thee:
> Living or dying, Lord, I would be Thine!

—Archbishop Francois de Salignac de la Mothe Fenelon (1651-1715)

75. 1. THE PROMISE: *"But my God shall supply all your need according to his riches in glory by Christ Jesus* (Philippians 4:19).

2. THE POINT: The child of God has a right to expect, especially in the light of the missionary-giving context of this passage, the provision of his every need. While the reception of "wants" is not assured, the getting of "needs" is guaranteed!

3. THE PROOF: It was winter in Toronto. Jonathan Goforth, the famous missionary, was in China but his wife, Rosalind, and children were in Canada. Just before the holidays, one of the boys came to his mother and complained: "Mother, just look at this, my best suit. The pants are above the ankles; and look at my sleeves—inches above the wrists! I have just been made secretary of the _____ Club of the University. How can I face these men, many of them important leaders? I'm the worst dressed man in the University."

One glance was enough to assure the truthfulness of his claim. Mrs. Goforth said, "My boy, there is no doubt it is a case of NEED. Let us stand on your father's great promise, 'My God shall supply all your need according to His riches in Christ Jesus.' I have no money, but I believe God will give the money for a suit if we trust Him."

The young man went off to school commenting about his mother's faith. In the meantime, Mrs. Goforth went to look for a suit. She found a lovely blue serge, but the price was $50. The thought "according to His riches" struck her mind, and she went home—fully expecting the Lord to provide for the suit!

Less than twenty-four hours later, a letter arrived from a woman in the United States whom Mrs. Goforth had met at a convention long years before. The letter explained the accompanying check as follows: "I am greatly interested in what you tell me of your children, particularly _____ (naming the boy needing the suit). Please buy something for him with the enclosed fifty dollars!"

The boy got the suit immediately!

4. THE POEM:
>Behold the lilies as they grow,
>   They neither toil nor spin,
>Yet human ne'er wore robes so fine
>   As God hath clothed them in.
>
>Could He, Who clothes the fragile flow'r,
>   Forget to clothe His own?
>In faith lay hold upon His pow'r,
>   To Him thy cares make known!
>
>—*B. Schlipf*

76.

1. THE PROMISE: *"For the hope which is laid up for you in heaven, whereof ye heard before in the word of the truth of the gospel"* (Colossians 1:6).

2. THE POINT: No hope is greater to man than the hope of Heaven. Fortunately, this hope is not merely "hopeful," it is a positive guarantee to every individual who has put his trust in Jesus Christ. Why? Because it is based upon "the word of the truth of the gospel."

3. THE PROOF: The late Harry Rimmer wrote a letter to the director of an international radio ministry and, before it reached its destination, God had called the warrior Home. This is what he had written:

"Next Sunday you are going to talk about Heaven. I am interested in that land because I have held a clear title to a bit of property there for about 50 years. I did not buy it. It was given to me without price. But the doner purchased it for me at a tremendous sacrifice. I am not holding it for speculation. It is not a vacant lot. For more than half a century I have been sending materials up to the greatest Architect of the universe who has been building a home for me which will never need remodeling or

> Beyond the farewell and the greeting,
> Beyond the pulse's fever beating,
> I shall be soon!
> Love, Rest and Home—Sweet Home!
> Lord, tarry not, but Come!
>
> —*Horatius Bonar* (1808-1889)

77.

1. THE PROMISE: *"For this cause also thank we God without ceasing, because, when ye received the word of God which ye heard of us, ye received it not as the word of men, but as it is in truth, the word of God, which effectually worketh also in you that believe"* (I Thessalonians 2:13).

2. THE POINT: The Word of God is a mighty, effective, powerful instrument which produces remarkable transformation in the life of one who believes. This is true in conversion; it is true in the Christian life.

3. THE PROOF: Peter Cartwright (1785-1872), an old-time circuit-riding Methodist preacher who, among other distinctions, had the "honor" of being defeated by Abraham Lincoln in an election for Congress, was conducting a camp meeting in Tennessee during the Fall of 1824 which met with considerable opposition from the forces of Satan. As is usual in such cases, the power of God was also manifested mightily.

In his autobiography, Cartwright says: "Connected with this meeting was another incident of thrilling interest, something like the following. There were two young men in this settlement of wealthy and respectable parentage, who were distantly related. They both were paying attention to a very wealthy young lady. Some jealousy about rivalship sprung up between them; they were mutually jealous of each other, and it spread like an eating cancer. They quarreled, and finally fought; both armed themselves, and each bound himself in a solemn oath to kill the other. Thus sworn, and armed with pistols and dirks, they attended camp meeting. I was acquainted with them, and apprised of the circumstances of this disagreeable affair.

"On Sunday, when I was addressing a large congregation, and was trying to enforce the terrors of the violated law of God, there was a visible power more than human rested on the congregation. Many fell under the preaching of the Word. In closing my discourse I called for mourners to come into the altar.

"Both these young men were in the congregation, and the Holy Spirit had convicted each of them; their murderous hearts quailed under the mighty power of God, and with dreadful feelings they made for the altar. One entered on the right, the other on the left. Each was perfectly ignorant of the other being there. I went deliberately to each of them, and took their deadly weapons from their bosoms, and carried them into the preachers' tent, and then returned and labored faithfully with them and others (for the altar was full) nearly all the afternoon and night.

"These young men had a sore struggle; but the great deep of their hearts was broken up, and they cried hard for mercy, and while I was kneeling by the side of one of them, just before the break of day, the Lord spoke peace to his wounded soul. He rose in triumph, and gave some thrilling shouts. I hastened to the other man, at the other side of the altar, and in less than fifteen minutes God powerfully blessed his soul, and he rose and shouted victory; and as these young men faced about they saw each other, and started simultaneously, met about midway of the altar, and instantly clasped each other in their arms.

"What a shout went up to Heaven from these young men, and almost the whole assembly that were present. There were a great many more who were converted that night, and, indeed, it was a night long to be remembered for the clear conversion of souls. One of these young men made an able itinerant preacher. He traveled a few years, had a brilliant career, and spread the holy fire wherever he went. He then fell sick, lingered a little while, and died triumphantly.

"There was a remarkable instance of the power of religion manifested in the change of these two young men. A few hours before they were sworn enemies, thirsting for each other's blood, but now all those murderous feelings were removed from them, and behold! their hearts were filled with love. 'Old things were done away, and all things became new.' "

Such is the power of the Word of God, which worketh effectually in them that believe!

4. THE POEM:
>The Word of God is like a sword
>   That pierces hearts, thus saith the Lord;
>And like a hammer, weighty, strong,
>   That can break up the rocks of sin and wrong.
>
>The Word of God is strong and sure,
>   Forevermore it shall endure,
>When oceans cease to kiss the shore,
>   When suns shall set to rise no more;
>
>'Mid crash of worlds it shall remain
>   Unshaken midst the starry rain,
>Upon its firm foundation strong,
>   I will plant my feet thro' the ages long.

78. 1. THE PROMISE: *"Faithful is he that calleth you, who also will do it"* (First Thessalonians 5:24).

2. THE POINT: God never calls but what He qualifies! Every Christian may be confident that whenever the Lord gives him a job to do, He will also give him the strength and ability to see that task through to a successful, victorious conclusion. In Christian service, the work is actually done by Him; we are simply the tools.

3. THE PROOF: Peter Cartwright was one of the original

circuit-riding Methodist preachers, born in the 18th century, who helped lay a spiritual foundation for this great nation. In October, 1803, when he was barely eighteen years of age, he felt impressed of God toward the ministry. His father objected but his mother encouraged him. After what he described as "a hard struggle," he yielded to the will of God.

Describing what happened next, he wrote in his *Autobiography:*

"At last I literally gave up the world, and started, bidding farewell to father and mother, brothers and sisters, and met Brother Lotspeich at an appointment in Logan County. He told me I must preach that night. This I had never done; mine was an exhorter's dispensation. I tried to beg off, but he urged me to make the effort. I went out and prayed fervently for aid from Heaven. All at once it seemed to me as if I could never preach at all, but I struggled in prayer. At length I asked God, if He had called me to preach, to give me aid that night, and give me one soul, that is, convert one soul under my preaching as evidence that I was called to this work.

"I went into the house, took my stand, gave out a hymn, sang, and prayed. I then rose, gave them for a text Isaiah 26:4, 'Trust ye in the Lord for ever: for in the Lord Jehovah is everlasting strength.' The Lord gave light, liberty, and power; the congregation was melted into tears. There was present a professed infidel. The word reached his heart by the Eternal Spirit. He was powerfully convicted, and, as I believe, soundly converted to God that night, and joined the church, and afterward became a useful member of the same."

Christian service can be summed up: we are *nothing;* He is *all!*

4. THE POEM:

>Master, to do great work for Thee my hand
> Is far too weak! Thou givest what may suit—
> Some little chips to cut with care minute,
>Or tint, or grave, or polish. Others stand
>Before their quarried marble fair and grand,
> And make a life-work of the great design
> Which Thou hast traced; or many, skilled, combine

    To build vast temples, gloriously planned;
Yet take the tiny stones which I have wrought,
   Just one by one as they were given by Thee,
Not knowing what came next in Thy wise thought;
Set each stone by Thy masterhand of grace,
   Form the mosaic as Thou wilt for me,
And in Thy temple pavement give it place.
                —*Frances Ridley Havergal* (1836-1879)

79. 1. THE PROMISE: *"Now the end of the commandment is love out of a pure heart, and of a good conscience, and of faith unfeigned"* (I Timothy 1:5, New Scofield Reference Bible).

2. THE POINT: The Living Word of the Living God is what revolutionizes the lives of those who hear and heed it. The more instruction from and through the Word, the more the disciple is changed into the image of God's dear Son, increasing in both faith and love.

3. THE PROOF: When Dr. Andrew Murray was ministering in his native South Africa, at Cape Town, he came in contact with a German deaconess who was working in an English church at Woodstock. Among her duties was an evening class for about a dozen Kaffirs who were preparing to be admitted into the church as members.

One night she talked to them about love. She particularly emphasized the importance of love for enemies. Turning to one of the men, she inquired as to whether his people had enemies. An enthusiastic affirmative response was immediately forthcoming.

"Who are they?"

He identified them as "the Fingoes," a people counted by the Kaffirs as dogs.

When she asked him if he could love the despised Fingo, his dogmatic answer was: "Me no' love Fingo. Me no' love Fingo."

As far as he was concerned, there were no "ifs," "ands" or "buts" about it: he simply could not love a Fingo! The new convert remained adamant in his conviction, even when the deaconess told him he could not go to the Lord's Table or be received into the fellowship of the church unless he changed his attitude.

He was a shaken man when he left for home and the following night in class he seemed most despondent and defeated. However, his position remained unchanged: "Me no' love Fingo!"

The others in his class were received into the church; he was not. Strangely, however, he continued to attend the class and it was evident to all that a bitter battle was going on within. The study of the Word of God was beginning to take its effect upon his stubborn heart. Finally, one happy night he appeared with obvious inward joy shining from his face and announced with glee: "Me now love Fingo!"

The Word of God had done its job.

4. THE POEM:

> This Holy Book I'd rather own
> Than all the gold and gems
> That e'er in monarch's coffers shone,
> Than all their diadems.
>
> Nay, were the seas one chrysolite,
> The earth one golden ball,
> And gems were all the stars of night,
> This Book outweighs them all.
>
> Ah, no, the soul ne'er found relief
> In glittering hoards of wealth;
> Gems dazzle not the eye of grief,
> Gold cannot purchase health.
>
> But here a blessed balm appears
> To heal the deepest woe;
> And those who read this Book in tears,
> Their tears shall cease to flow.

80.

1. THE PROMISE: *"For the word of God is quick, and powerful, and sharper than any twoedged sword, piercing even to the dividing asunder of soul and spirit, and of the joints and marrow, and is a discerner of the thoughts and intents of the heart. Neither is there any creature that is not manifest in his sight: but all things are naked and opened unto the eyes of him with whom we have to do"* (Hebrews 4:12,13).

2. THE POINT: The wonderful Word of Almighty God is able to pierce the hardest, toughest heart of the coldest, most indifferent sinner who ever lived. Neither is there any respect of persons with its power; old and young, rich and poor, unknown or illustrious—it is able to smite effectively.

3. THE PROOF: In one of his last addresses at England's famed Keswick Convention, the late Dr. Arthur T. Pierson related the case of Russia's Baron Uxhill, an infidel of the agnostic stripe. It seems that some uneducated, simple evangelists had visited the farm next to the baron's estate and amazing results had taken place among the workmen. So impressed was he with what had happened that, although he cared absolutely nothing for the Christian faith or the Christ it exalted, he told the preachers: "Come on my estate. Anything that will make drunken men sober, and indolent men industrious, and immoral men moral, and dishonest men honest, I want to have on my estate."

It was strictly a business proposition with the baron. He realized the financial worth it would be to him if his workers were transformed. The evangelists accepted his invitation and such a notable work was accomplished that Uxhill built a chapel on his grounds for them to use.

When it came time to dedicate the chapel, the worshipers invited the benefactor to be present. He said, "I do not take any stock in what you are saying and doing, but I will come." And he was there.

During the dedication ceremonies they presented him with a

Bible and asked him to read it. Impressed with what he had seen and heard, Baron Uxhill took the Word of God home with him and began, curiously at first, to read it. Eventually he came to I Peter 2:24, "Who his own self bare our sins in his own body on the tree, that we, being dead to sins, should live unto righteousness: by whose stripes ye were healed."

Baron Uxhill dropped to his knees, lifting his heart to God and crying: "And *mine* also!" *Immediately he was converted.* Later he made a trip to the United States, raising money to build additional chapels for workmen.

4. THE POEM:

>Where childhood needs a standard
>   Or youth a beacon light,
>Where sorrow sighs for comfort
>   Or weakness longs for night,
>Bring forth the Holy Bible,
>   The Bible! Here it stands!
>Resolving all life's problems
>   And meeting its demands.
>Though sophistry conceal it,
>   The Bible! There it stands!
>Though Pharisees profane it,
>   Its influence expands.
>It fills the world with fragrance
>   Whose sweetness never cloys,
>It lifts our eyes to Heaven,
>   It heightens human joys.
>Despised and torn in pieces,
>   By infidels decried—
>The thunderbolts of hatred
>   The haughty cynics pride—
>All these have railed against it
>   In this and other lands,
>Yet dynasties have fallen
>   And still the Bible stands!
>To Paradise a highway,
>   The Bible! Here it stands!
>Its promises unfailing,
>   Nor grievous its commands.
>It points man to the Savior,
>   The lover of his soul;

Salvation is its watchword,
Eternity its goal!
—*James Martin Gray* (1851-1935)

81.

1. **THE PROMISE:** *"We have not an high priest which cannot be touched with the feeling of our infirmities; but was in all points tempted like as we are, yet without sin. Let us therefore come boldly unto the throne of grace, that we may obtain mercy, and find grace to help in time of need"* (Hebrews 4:15,16).

2. THE POINT: Christians have a hidden source of strength, a secret for gaining victory, for turning defeat and despair into triumph and gladness. We may enter the presence of the One who has conquered every foe, at any time of need, confident that His mercy and grace will abundantly be given.

3. THE PROOF: Adoniram Judson is one of the all-time great heroes of the Christian faith. A pioneer missionary to Burma, the hardships and difficulties he faced and endured are almost unfathomable to the modern mind. On one occasion, in 1832, he was imprisoned at Rangoon and subjected to terrible daily tortures.

In fact, one day things were so bad he pleaded with the officer in charge, "Cast me into the water and let me drown; I have sojourned in this land and done my best for Christ, but it has come to naught; let me drown!"

That season of despair was only fleeting, however, and in another moment he was adding, "No, no. I must cheerfully fill the place God has appointed me!" And so he did, eventually winning thousands of souls to Christ in that land.

4. THE POEM:
> Lonely I trod the moor.
> Black was the sky;

There was no man nor beast,
No creature nigh;
Only Grief dogged my steps,
Grief and Despair.
Fled I to north or south,
Still they were there.
Darkness had compassed me,
Gone was my sight,
Well-nigh my feet had slipped. . .
Then shone a light,
Then spoke a Voice to me,
Gentle and sweet,
"O thy poor bleeding heart,
O thy torn feet!
I am thy Shepherd kind,
Thou art My sheep.
Safely within My arms
Rest now and sleep."
Then slunk those wolves away,
Grief and Despair. . .
Suddenly morning broke,
Rosy and fair!

—*Martha Snell Nicholson*

82.

1. THE PROMISE: *"For God is not unrighteous to forget your work and labour of love, which ye have shewed toward his name, in that ye have ministered to the saints, and do minister"* (Hebrews 6:10).

2. THE POINT: A basic Bible principle, found repeatedly, is that faithful service for God will be honored. In fact, anything less would be considered an act of unrighteousness by Him. He told Eli, "Them that honor me I will honor" (I Samuel 2:30), and our Saviour assured His disciples, "if any man serve me, him will my Father honour" (John 12:26).

3. THE PROOF: The great evangelist of the late 19th century, Dwight Lyman Moody, was a man who honored the Word of God in his preaching. He *believed* it, *exalted* it, *preached* it and *defended* it. Immense crowds filled the auditoriums where he spoke. On "Chicago Day" at the World's Fair, when even the theaters closed down because everyone was expected to be at the Fair grounds, Moody ordered the large Central Music Hall engaged for continuous services from 9 a.m. until 6 p.m. They did as he instructed—although everyone else thought it would be a total failure—and Dr. R. A. Torrey, who reported the incident, said that when he went to the building at noon, the crowds were jammed so tightly around the front that he was compelled to climb through a back window in order to reach the platform.

During the same World's Fair, while Moody was consistently drawing thousands to hear him preach the unsearchable riches of Christ, the Fair's famous World's Congress of Religions asked a very gifted man of letters from the East to address the Congress. The noted divine considered it the honor of a lifetime and immediately went to work on his paper. After rewriting it several times he sent it to some select friends for constructive criticism and suggestions. When they returned the paper, he rewrote it, incorporating the suggestions they had made which seemed wise, then sent it on another round for further criticism. After that he wrote it a final time and anxiously awaited the hour of its delivery.

When the "big day" eventually arrived, the learned clergyman waited outside the platform door until the exact hour struck, then proudly marched to the pulpit to face a "multitude" of two men and eleven women! But there was not an auditorium in Chicago that same day which could have held the crowds who would have flocked to hear Moody at any hour, day or night.

4. THE POEM:
>How dear to my heart is the church of my childhood
> Where I took my first step in the straight, narrow way;
>The little white church near the thick-tangled wildwood
> Where I went with my mother on every Lord's day.
>There was no large pipe organ, no high-paid soprano;

The singing was scarcely the best ever heard;
But the man in the pulpit, divinely commissioned,
  Poured out his whole soul in proclaiming God's Word.
An old-fashioned preacher, a real Bible preacher,
  A Spirit-filled preacher who honored the Word.

How thrilling it was just to see him in action,
  This soldier of Christ, with his keen, trusty "sword,"
Who wielded his weapon with zeal and devotion,
  And backed up each thrust with a "Thus saith the Lord!"
No uncertain sound ever came from his trumpet,
  His hearers were moved—yes, convicted and stirred;
And, bowing the knee in wet-eyed confession,
  Accepted the truth as revealed in the Word
By this old-fashioned preacher, this full Gospel preacher,
  This Spirit-taught preacher who honored the Word.

Sometimes, when I list to the ramifications
  Of science, that twist my poor brain out of shape,
Or hear the consensus of scholarship's findings,
  Regarding our old friend, the antropoid ape;
As my mind reels, confused with drives, plans, and programs,
  And world federations toward which we are stirred—
Sociology, politics, internationalism,
  I sigh for the sermons my infancy heard
From this old-fashioned preacher, this soul-stirring preacher,
  This heart-warming preacher who honored God's Word.

83. 1. THE PROMISE: *"Wherefore he is able also to save them to the uttermost that come unto God by him, seeing he ever liveth to make intercession for them"* (Hebrews 7:25).

2. THE POINT: With God there are no impossible cases. He is able to save and to save thoroughly, from the guttermost to the uttermost. Our Living Lord takes dead sinners and transforms them into living saints. The work of redemption is a miracle in which He delights!

3. THE PROOF: Everyone called him "Jimmy the Rat." Somehow, when he was only a 16-year-old farm boy in Indiana, he had been introduced to opium. Before he was out of his teens he had sunk to the depths of addiction's depravity, earning the title "the Rat" because of the long cupboard shelf he used for a bedchamber.

Eventually he ended up in a Clark Street dope den in Chicago, run by a Mongolian Chinaman. To a passerby, the establishment was merely a Chinese laundry operated by a John Lee, but down in the cellar, housed in wooden bunk beds which lined both sides of the room in double tiers, the addicts were confined. Jimmy the Rat, along with other human derelicts, lived only for the oblivion produced by the shots of morphine, heroin, opium and cocaine. He was a white-faced, shrunken skeleton wrapped in skin, unloved and unwanted by society.

One Sunday afternoon he heard a group from the Pacific Garden Mission singing outside in the street:

> **Though I forget Him and wander away,**
> **Still He doth love me wherever I stray;**
> **Back to His dear loving arms would I flee,**
> **When I remember that Jesus loves me.**
> **I am so glad that Jesus loves me,**
> **Jesus loves me, Jesus loves me;**
> **I am so glad that Jesus loves me,**
> **Jesus loves even me.**

Quietly, trying to slip out without being detected, Jimmy unlocked the door and made his way to the open air. Standing on the mission's Gospel Wagon was a burly giant who was testifying: "This here Pacific Garden Mission crowd prayed me back to a decent life and—"

At that moment a hand reached out from inside the establishment and dragged the hungry-hearted listener back in. Fearing Jimmy might get religion and inform on their illicit traffic in dope, a huge Chinaman started to beat him to a pulp before he "croaked and the police started investigating the dead lobby gow." Thinking the task had been accomplished, they carried him from the opium den and dumped him behind a stack of lumber on a side street. Somehow Jimmy got to his feet and staggered to the mission. Arriving just as the congregation was concluding a song, he started up the aisle crying, "I want somebody to pray for me!"

Christ saved Him and saved Him completely! Later he returned to Indiana, married, and became a successful farmer and father. While he continued giving a glorious testimony regarding the saving grace of God in Christ, he eventually dropped his nickname because of his children. They, instead, grew to maturity praising God in prayer, "Thank You for the Pacific Garden Mission where daddy learned to know Jesus."

4. THE POEM:

>**My robes were once all stained with sin,**
>**I knew not how to make them clean**
>**Until a voice said, sweet and low,**
>**"Go wash, I will make them white as snow."**
>
>**That promise, "Whosoever will,"**
>**Included me, includes me still.**
>**I came, and ever since I know**
>**His blood has made me white as snow.**
>
>**I have washed my robes in Jesus' blood**
>**And He has made them white as snow.**

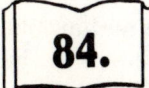

84. 1. THE PROMISE: *"Let your conversation be without covetousness; and be content with such things as ye have: for he hath said, I will never leave thee, nor forsake thee. So that we may boldly say, The Lord is my helper, and I will not fear what man shall do unto me"* (Hebrews 13:5,6).

2. THE POINT: The child of God has his Father's guarantee that his needs will be met. He has the pledge of his Redeemer's presence until the very end and can boldly trust Him to supply

every need and to answer every problem.

3. THE PROOF: Late in the 19th century, the following appeared in *The Sunday School Times*: "Among the officers of a church in New England, of which the writer was pastor some years ago, was Deacon C_____. For years of his Christian life he had frugally maintained his little family on a portion of his moderate salary. The remainder he had sacredly devoted to Christian uses. He was a systematic beneficence society in efficient working order. As a consequence, while his living was on a modest scale, his giving was done in princely style. From his charities you would have supposed him to be a millionaire. He did a larger business for the world's welfare, with the Lord as 'silent partner,' and on a smaller capital, than any other man I ever knew.

"There was much querying over this bold policy of Deacon C_____. It seemed like suicidal folly to live with no provision for the future. The young men in his Bible class used to ask, 'Now, Deacon, would you advise us to go on in your style, spending or giving every dollar, and never taking death or old age into account?'

" 'Why,' he would answer, ' "according to your faith be it unto you." Can you enjoy this kind of life? That is the question. Can you rest on God, with nothing else on which to rest, as you would on $50,000 worth of bonds? Can you believe, clear down to the bottom of your soul, and without a quiver of doubt, that the Lord will take care of you? If you can, then do it, and God will bless you in it. But if you are going into this way of living as you would into a lion's cage, trembling all over; if you see nothing but starvation at the end of it; if you are to be scourged into it by the lash of conscience—to have no peace or joy or liberty in it—then I advise you not to make the venture.'

"And there were few or none who did make the venture. The question often went from mouth to mouth, 'How will the deacon come out with his experiment? How will it strike him when too old to work?'

"I removed from the town while Deacon C_____ was in the prime of his powers. Years passed on, and I heard nothing of him or his fortunes. But at last, shortly after his death, came a letter from an excellent lady, in the same church, which read substantially as follows: 'By the way, it will interest you to know how Deacon C_____ came out at last with his life of faith. Some two years before his death he was struck with paralysis and rendered helpless. The E_____ Company (a large corporation in whose service he was) esteemed him so highly that, for a year, they continued his salary. Then it fell off to half pay for about the same period. At last his income ceased altogether. But his cheerfulness never abated; his confidence that God would provide for him never seemed clouded.

" 'He was brought finally to his last hundred dollars when the time arrived for his annual contribution to the American Board. Without hesitation he divided the amount with the Lord, giving $50 to the cause of missions. So matters stood when an aged aunt of his, who had died suddenly, was found to have left him $11,000, which provided for him through the remainder of his life.' "

Thank God, **it works!**

4. THE POEM:

> Child of My love, lean hard,
> And let Me feel the pressure of thy care.
> I know thy burden, child; I shaped it,
> Poised it in Mine own hand, made no proportion
> In its weight to thine unaided strength;
> For even as I laid it on, I said,
> I shall be near, and while he leans on Me
> This burden shall be Mine, not his;
> So shall I keep My child within the circling arms
> Of Mine own love. Here lay it down, nor fear
> To impose it upon a shoulder which upholds
> The government of worlds. Yet closer come,
> Thou art not near enough; I would embrace thy care
> So I might feel My child reposing on My breast.
> Thou lovest Me? I know it. Doubt not then;
> But loving Me, lean hard.
>
> —*Paul Pastnor*

85.

1. THE PROMISE: *"If any of you lack wisdom, let him ask of God, that giveth to all men liberally, and upbraideth not; and it shall be given him"* (James 1:5).

2. THE POINT: God, the Author of wisdom, is also the principal Source of wisdom! How natural and logical, therefore, to turn to Him when wisdom in any field is needed. This promise is not only good for direction in the spiritual life, it is one intended by the Redeemer for use in every area of the Christian's experience and walk.

3. THE PROOF: William Haldeman is an Indianapolis product who made good in more ways than one! After graduating from Shortridge High School [he was born again during his junior year], he went on to Purdue University, eventually receiving his Master's Degree in physics from that institution. Within two weeks after clutching that prized sheepskin to his bosom, Bill had been hired by the Navy at one of its ordinance plants and given the extremely difficult job of working on a new solid state analog computer. Specifically, he was to figure a way to make such a computer use physical variables like distance, temperature and speed in airplane flights to compute target locations. At the time, although numerous agencies had worked on the problem, it was an "unknown" and "unanswered" question.

Haldeman approached his task scientifically by touring a number of large computer concerns, seeking to learn what others had discovered or had attempted. His fruitless search brought him home empty-handed and discouraged. Nothing he tried in his own experiments brought a solution any closer.

So Bill went to a Higher Source. Going to his office early one morning, he began to wrestle and plead with God to show him the solution. As he did, he promised again that he would "honor Him in my life."

What happened? In less than two weeks he had the answer about how to match the components. In less than a month the computers were in production and an aviation milestone had been reached.

What did Bill do? For the next half-year this gifted scientist, now associated with the United States Manned Spacecraft Center in Houston, toured the country explaining to scientific groups how the problem had been solved through divine intervention, giving the glory to God.

4. THE POEM:

>Awake, my soul, and with the sun
>   Thy daily stage of duty run;
>Shake off dull sloth, and joyful rise
>   To pay the morning sacrifice.
>
>Wake, and lift up thyself, my heart,
>   And with the angels bear thy part,
>Who all night long unwearied sing
>   High praise to the Eternal King.
>
>Lord! I my vows to Thee renew;
>   Scatter my sins like morning dew;
>Guard my first springs of thought and will,
>   And with Thyself my spirit fill.
>
>Direct, control, suggest, this day,
>   All I design, or do, or say;
>That all my powers, with all their might,
>   In Thy sole glory may unite.
>
>—*Bishop Thomas Ken* (1637-1711)

86.

1. THE PROMISE: *"Hearken, my beloved brethren, Hath not God chosen the poor of this world rich in faith, and heirs of the kingdom which he hath promised to them that love him?"* (James 2:5).

2. THE POINT: Inheritance in His kingdom is not the only reward for loving our Lord. He has gifted His own with a wealth

of faith, especially those who must be classified as "the poor of this world."

3. THE PROOF: In the late 18th century there was a Negro slave by the name of Newport Gardner. Possibly this remarkable African got his given name from the locality and his surname from his owner, since he was owned by a man named Gardner who lived in Newport, Rhode Island.

A devoutly religious man, this humble believer worked hard in the area of self-education. And he worked equally as hard toward eventually obtaining his freedom and freedom for his family. In his biography of Dr. Samuel Hopkins, Professor Park gives the following account:

"He was allowed to labor for his own profit during whatever time he might gain by extra diligence. The slave devoted all this gained time to procuring the means of liberating himself and family. He was finally advised by a deacon of Mr. Hopkins' church to spend this time in fasting and prayer for his liberation; he was assured of more rapid success in this course than in that of manual labor.

"Accordingly, having gained a day, this pious Negro, without communicating his plan to any but Mr. Hopkins and two or three Christian friends, spent that day in secret fasting and prayer, that he might obtain his freedom. His master, totally ignorant of his slave's occupation, sent for him about four o'clock in the afternoon, but was told that Newport was engaged for himself, this being his gained day.

" 'No matter; call him,' said Captain Gardner.

"After some hesitation the slave was called and his owner gave him a paper, on which was written: 'I, Caleb Gardner, of Newport, Rhode Island, do this day manumit and release forever, Newport Gardner, his wife and children,' etc., etc., adding some conditions which could easily be complied with. The slave received his manumission with gratitude to his owner, but with still deeper gratitude to his all-wise Disposer above, who had signally answered his request for freedom, even before he had finished his supplication."

4. THE POEM:

>Thy thoughts are good, and Thou art kind,
>   E'en when we think it not;
>How many an anxious, faithless mind
>   Sits grieving o'er its lot,
>And frets and pines by day and night,
>As God had lost it out of sight,
>   And all its wants forgot.
>
>Ah, no! God ne'er forgets His own,
>   His heart is far too true;
>He ever seeks their good alone,
>   His love is daily new,
>And though thou deem that things go ill,
>Yet He is just and holy still,
>   In all things He can do.
>
>The Lord is ever close and near
>   To those who keep His Word;
>Whene'er they cry to Him in fear,
>   Their prayer is surely heard;
>He knoweth well who love Him well;
>His love shall yet their clouds dispel,
>   And grant the hope deferred.
>
>   —*Paul Gerhardt* (1607-1676)

87.

1. THE PROMISE: *"The effectual fervent prayer of a righteous man availeth much"* (James 5:16).

2. THE POINT: When a man who is "right" gets hold of God in earnest, compassionate intercession, the possibilities for good are almost unlimited!

3. THE PROOF: The noted evangelist, Charles G. Finney, told of a godly man in the western part of New York State who,

though on the threshold of death with tuberculosis, literally wrought miracles through the power of importunate prayer. Finney wrote:

"He was a poor man and had been sick for years. An unconverted merchant in the place had a kind heart and used to send him, now and then, something for his comfort, or for his family. He felt grateful, but could make no return for the kindness, as he wanted to. At length he determined that the best return he could make would be to pray for his friend. He began to pray, his soul kindled, and he got hold of God. There was no revival, but by-and-by, to the astonishment of everybody, this merchant came right out on the Lord's side. The fire kindled all over the place; a powerful revival followed, and a multitude were converted.

"This poor man lingered in this way for several years and died. After his death, I visited the place and his widow put into my hands his diary. Among other things he said in his diary: 'I am acquainted with about thirty ministers and churches.' He then went on to set apart certain hours in the day and week to pray for each of these ministers and churches and, also, certain seasons for praying for certain missionary stations.

"Then followed, under different dates, such facts as these: 'Today,' naming the date, 'I have been enabled to offer what I call the prayer of faith for the outpouring of the Spirit on _____ Church, and I trust in God there will soon be a revival there.' Under another date: 'I have today been enabled to offer which I call the prayer of faith for such a church, and trust there will soon be a revival there.' Thus he had gone over a great number of churches, recording the fact that he had prayed for them in faith. Revival after revival followed in the several places in the order in which he had prevailed in prayer, both at home and in mission churches!"

4. THE POEM:
>Pray for my soul. More things are wrought by prayer
>Than this world dreams of. Wherefore let thy voice
>Rise like a fountain for me night and day.

> For what are men better than sheep or goats,
> That nourish a blind life within the brain,
> If, knowing God, they lift not hands of prayer
> Both for themselves, and those who call them friend?
> For so the whole round earth is every way
> Bound by gold chains about the feet of God.
> —*Alfred Tennyson* (1809-1892)

88. 1. THE PROMISE: *"In the same manner, ye wives, be in subjection to your own husbands that, if any obey not the word, they also may without the word be won by the behavior of the wives. While they behold your chaste conduct coupled with fear"* (I Peter 3:1,2 *New Scofield Reference Bible*).

2. THE POINT: Christian wives, if they really mean business and are willing to pay the price, can win unconverted husbands to Christ—even if those unbelieving mates refuse to attend church or listen to the Word of God. The "winning" is done through the life lived by the wife!

3. THE PROOF: The following is an entry in the *Autobiography of George Muller* for the year 1835:

"March 18. This afternoon we arrived at Basle, where we were very kindly received by the brethren.—During my stay there I attended one day a meeting at which a venerable pious clergyman expounded the Greek New Testament to several brethren, who purposed to give themselves to missionary service. The passage to which this dear aged brother had them come, in the original of the New Testament, was I Peter 3:1,2. . .After this aged brother had expounded the passage, he related a circumstance which had occurred in his own days, and under his own eyes at Basle, which has appeared to me so encouraging for those children of God who have unbelieving relatives, and especially for sisters in the Lord who have unbelieving husbands; and which at the same time is such a beautiful illustration of I Peter 3:1, that I judge it desirable to insert the narrative of this fact here. I will do so exactly as I remember it.—There lived at Basle an opulent citizen, whose wife was a believer, but he himself feared not the Lord. His practice was to spend his evenings in a winehouse, where he would often tarry till eleven, twelve, or even one o'clock. On such occasions his wife always used to send her servants to bed, and sat up herself to await the return of her husband. When at last he came, she used to receive him most kindly, never reproach him in the least either at the time or afterwards, nor complain at all on account of his late hours, by which she was kept from reasonable rest. Moreover, if it should be needful to assist him in undressing himself, when he had drunk to excess, she would do this also in a very kind and meek way. Thus it went on for a long time. One evening, this gentleman was again, as usual, in a winehouse, and having tarried there with his merry companions till midnight, he said to them: 'I bet that if we go to my house, we will find my wife sitting up and waiting for me, and she herself will come to the door and receive us very kindly; and if I ask her to prepare us a supper, she will do it at once without the least murmur, or unkind expression, or look.' His companions in sin did not believe his statement. At last, however, after some more conversation about this strange statement (as it appeared to them), it was agreed that they would all go to see this kind wife. Accordingly they went, and, after they had knocked, found the door immediately opened by the lady herself, and they were all courteously and kindly received by her. The party having entered, the master of the house asked his wife to prepare supper for them, which she, in the meekest way, at once agreed to do; and, after awhile, supper was served by herself without the least sign of dissatisfaction, or murmur, or complaint. Having now prepared all for the company, she retired from the party to her room. When she left the party, one of the gentlemen said: 'What a wicked and cruel man you are, thus to torment so kind a wife.' He then took his hat and stick, and, without touching a morsel of the supper, went away. Another made a similar remark, and left, without touching the supper. Thus one after another left, till they were all gone, without tasting the supper. The master of the house was now left alone, and the Spirit of God brought before him all his dreadful wickedness, and especially his great sins toward his wife; and the party had not left the house half an hour, before he went to his wife's room, requesting her to pray for him, told her that he felt himself a great sinner, and asked her forgiveness for all his behavior towards her. From that time he became a disciple of the Lord Jesus.

"Observe here, dear reader, the following points in particular, which I affectionately commend to your consideration: (1) The wife acted in accordance with I Peter 3:1. She kept her place as being in subjection, and the Lord owned. (2) She reproached not her husband, but meekly and kindly served him when he used to come home. (3) She did not allow the servants to sit up for their master, but sat up herself, thus honoring him as her head and superior, and concealed also, as far as she was able, her husband's shame from the servants. (4) In all probability a part of those hours, during which she had to sit up, was spent in prayer for her husband, or in reading the Word of God, to gather fresh strength for all the trials connected with her position. (5) Be not discouraged if you have to suffer from unconverted relatives. Perhaps very shortly the Lord may give you the desire of your heart, and answer your prayer for them; but in the meantime seek to commend the truth, not by reproaching them on account of their behavior towards you, but by manifesting towards them the meekness, gentleness, and kindness of the Lord Jesus Christ."

4. THE POEM:
>Oh, if the selfish knew how much they lost,
> What would they not endeavor, not endure,
> To imitate, as far as in them lay,
>Him who His wisdom and His power employs
>In making others happy?
>
>—*William Cowper* (1731-1800)

89. 1. THE PROMISE: *"And above all things have fervent love among yourselves; for love shall cover the multitude of sins"* (I Peter 4:8, *New Scofield Reference Bible).*

2. THE POINT: No man is without sin; all of us have our faults and our imperfections. Unless we cherish love continually the one toward another, disharmony, division, disruption and dishonor to the name of Christ and His church will be inevitable. Not only so, but passionate, intense love will so blanket a brother's "mass of sins," he will earnestly seek his restoration when he goes astray.

3. THE PROOF: The beloved "Apostle of Love" is certainly a case in point. The story, which is accepted as fact as nearly as any account of secular history can be, is related by Clement of Alexandria.

It seems that John, while ministering at Ephesus long before he was exiled to the Isle of Patmos, had adopted a fine young man of seemingly great potential in both character and intellect. On one occasion, when it was necessary for him to leave Ephesus on a journey for his Master, John left the youth in the care of a leader in the Ephesian church. Instead of helping the lad advance in spiritual growth, however, the slothful guardian failed miserably in his duties.

In a short time the son had fallen in with evil companions and dropped quickly from one excess to another. Eventually he formed his own band of robbers and filled the entire countryside with fear. All his former training was seemingly forgotten and abandoned.

When John arrived back at Ephesus, he hurried immediately to the bishop's home and inquired for the return of "the precious deposit he had left in his hands." Not understanding what John meant until he explained that he had returned for his son, the bishop was forced to acknowledge with downcast eyes what had happened.

John cried out in despair, "Alas! alas! to what a guardian have

I trusted our brother!" Then, calling for a horse, he rode the steed in haste to the forest where the bandit gang resided. At first his adopted son tried to flee from his presence, but John cried out for him to stop with such fervent entreaties that he finally did.

After a short, brokenhearted appeal from the lips of John, the prodigal son burst into agonizing tears of repentance, imploring John to forgive him. Even as he spoke, he hid his right hand—used so repeatedly in the vilest of crimes—in his bosom. But John, dropping to his knees before his adopted son, seized the erring hand and bathed it with scalding tears as his lips caressed it. And he remained in that position of love and entreaty until the erring son had been reconciled with both Heaven and himself. Love had succeeded where all else would have failed.

4. THE POEM:

> 'Tis love that makes our willing feet
>   In swift obedience move.
> When, free from envy, scorn, and pride,
>   Our wishes all above,
> Each can his brother's failing hide,
>   And show a brother's love!
> Love is the golden chain that binds
>   The happy souls above;
> And he's an heir of Heaven that finds
>   His bosom glow with love.

90.

1. THE PROMISE: *"Casting all your care upon him; for he careth for you"* (I Peter 5:7).

2. THE POINT: God intends His dear children to "unload" all their anxieties upon Him because He is so definitely interested in every minute detail of their lives. Kenneth S. Wuest says the latter phrase may be translated literally, "for you are His concern." S. D. Gordon suggests: "He has you on His heart."

3. THE PROOF: James H. Smith tells of a woman of very humble circumstances who paid a considerable amount of money to a local businessman. After some time, the latter presented her with a statement, saying the sum had never been paid. While she was positive the bill had been settled, she could find no receipt to prove it. The dishonest merchant threatened to have the sheriff foreclose on her property unless she satisfied his claim at once.

The distraught lady went immediately to God in prayer, crying, "Oh, my Heavenly Father, Thou knowest the distress I am in. Thou knowest that it will ruin me if my little cottage and place are sold. Oh, my Heavenly Father, undertake for me! I know I paid that man. My Father, have mercy on me and find this receipt for me."

It was a beautiful sunny day and, as she arose from her knees, a butterfly flew in her open door, followed quickly by an excited child seeking to capture the beautiful insect. The youth made a swipe at the butterfly but the force of the movement knocked it behind a cupboard. Then, in the typical temper-tantrum style of the immature, the child began screaming for the cupboard to be moved. About that time a neighbor appeared, inquiring as to the child's trouble.

"Well," the lady replied, "a butterfly flew in and the child wants to get it. However, it is behind that heavy cupboard there, and I cannot move it."

"Oh," said the woman, "let me help you move it." Together they managed to move the bulky cupboard away from the wall and, as they did so, something fluttered to the floor. It was a piece of paper which had been knocked behind the cupboard and had wedged between it and the wall. When the old lady picked it up, she held in her hands the receipted bill!

4. THE POEM:
>"Jesus lover of my soul"
>Bids me in His bosom stay,
>And though billows round me roll,
>I am safely hid away;

For He holds me in His arms,
   Quite beyond the tempest's reach
And He whispers to my heart,
   Words unknown to human speech.

"Other refuge have I none,"
   He, my habitation is;
Here no evil can befall
   I am kept in perfect peace.
I am covered all day long
   With the shadow of His wing;
Dwell in safety through the night,
   Waking, this is what I sing:

"Thou, O Christ, art all I want,"
   Rests my helpless soul on Thee;
Thou wilt never leave alone
   Nor forget to comfort me.
Thou hast saved my soul from death,
   Thou hast scattered doubts and fears,
And the sunshine of Thy face
   Sweetly drieth all my tears.

"Thou of life the fountain art,"
   Thou dost wash me white as snow;
I'm content to dwell apart
   From all else, Thy love to know.
Blessed Son of Righteousness
   I so love to look on Thee,
That my eyes are growing blind
   To the things once dear to me.

91. 1. THE PROMISE: *"According as his divine power hath given unto us all things that pertain unto life and godliness, through the knowledge of him that hath called us to glory and virtue: Whereby are given unto us exceeding great and precious promises: that by these ye might be partakers of the divine* *nature, having escaped the corruption that is in the world through lust"* (II Peter 1:3,4).

2. THE POINT: The child of God is perfectly equipped, his Heavenly Father having made every provision for every emergency. No matter the trial, the test, the persecution, the suffering, the opposition, the temptation, there are "exceeding great and precious promises" more than sufficient to meet the crisis. While those promises are not always appropriated by the troubled saint, they are there nonetheless.

3. THE PROOF: When the late Donald Grey Barnhouse was living in France as a student, the Lord enabled him to win a local young lady to Christ who later married a pastor in the south of France. Once, when she was visiting in the Barnhouse home, she saw them taking verses from their "promise box." [It contained about 200 promises from the Word of God, each printed on heavy paper and curled into cylinders.]

The visitor was so intrigued that she laboriously made her own promise box, writing out by hand the same promises in French. It became an integral part of the family life in the pastor's home, and whenever they needed a special word of comfort, they went to the box.

One memorable time of crisis came during the war. The only food in the house consisted of potato peelings obtained from a restaurant. The children, whose clothing was practically in rags and whose shoes were worn completely through, were hungry and crying for nourishment.

Almost in desperation the young pastor's wife turned to the beloved promise box, crying to God as she did so: "Lord, I have such a great need. Is there a promise here that is really for me? Show me, O Lord, what promise I can have in this time of famine, nakedness, peril and the sword!"

So blinded was she by the tears streaming down her cheeks that, in grasping for the box, she sent it flying. Immediately she was showered with promises from head to foot—in her hair, on her lap, around her in the chair and on the floor. Not a single promise remained in the box! In a moment the sorrow had turned into joy, the defeat into victory, and the despair into encouragement as the blessed realization struck her that "all the promises of God in him are yea, and in him Amen, unto the glory of God by us" (II Corinthians 1:20).

4. THE POEM:
>When my heart was vex'd with care,
>Fill'd with tears well-nigh despair;
>When, with watching many a night,
>On me fell pale sickness' blight;
>>When my courage fail'd me fast,
>>Camest Thou, my God, at last,
>>And my woes were quickly past.
>>>*—Paul Gerhardt* (1607-1676)

92.

1. THE PROMISE: *"If ye know that he is righteous, ye know that every one that doeth righteousness is born of him"* (I John 2:29).

2. THE POINT: One of the evidences of the new birth in a life is the revolutionary change in that life. Before, interested in the flesh; after, interested in the Spirit. Things once loved are hated; things once despised are loved. Regeneration manifests itself in "doing righteousness."

3. THE PROOF: In the fascinating autobiography of Gipsy Smith, he relates an experiance of a lovely young woman who was converted in one of his meetings at the Wharton Street Methodist Episcopal Church of Philadelphia. Smith wrote:

"When I think of Old Wharton Street my mind at once recalls a beautiful story of a young girl there. She was a bright creature, fond of society, fond of pleasure.

"The story begins some weeks before my mission. A dance was to be held at a friend's house, and the girl was anxious to go to it.

Her mother said, 'Lilly, if you get converted and join the church you may go to the dance.'

"Shortly after this Lilly joined the church and she said to her mother, 'Now that I have joined the church, Mother, I may go to the dance, may I not?''

" 'Oh, but, my dear, you have joined the church, it is true; but you are not converted. You know very well that you are not, and we can see very well that you are not.'

"Nothing more was said on that occasion. Presently I came to the church to conduct a mission, and Lilly was persuaded to attend. One night her proud, wayward heart was subdued and broken in penitence, and she gave herself to God. There was still a week or two before the dance. Her mother knew of the great change in her daughter's life, and she noticed also that Lilly had ceased to speak about the dance.

"One day she said, 'Lilly, what about this dance; it comes off next week. Are you going?'

" 'Oh, Mother dear,' said the sweet girl, throwing her arms round her mother's neck and shedding tears of joy, 'I have given my heart to the Lord, and I have no longer any desire to go to the dance.'

"Mother and daughter both shed happy tears of gratitude to God."

4. THE POEM:

> 'Tis not the wide phylactery,
>   Nor stubborn fast, nor stated prayers,
> That make us saints; we judge the tree
>   By what it bears.
>
> And when a man can live apart
>   From works, on theologic trust,
> I know the blood about his heart
>   Is dry as dust.

—*Alice Cary* (1820-1871)

93. 1. THE PROMISE: *"Beloved, if our heart condemn us not, then have we confidence toward God. And whatsoever we ask, we receive of him, because we keep his commandments, and do those things that are pleasing in his sight"* (I John 3:21,22).

2. THE POINT: Self-condemnation comes through disobedience to the Word of God. On the other hand, obedience to His commandments frees the heart from this condemnation. With an uncondemned heart, the child of God can approach the throne of grace with the absolute confidence that his prayer will be both heard and answered.

3. THE PROOF: D. L. Moody, insisting that he ran his schools by faith, nonetheless was a confirmed beggar when it came to asking Christians of means for support when needed. On one occasion, early in his ministry, Moody had gone to the millionaire, Cyrus H. McCormick, and asked for a thousand dollars for his mission school. First complaining that Moody had been touching him "rather hard of late," the industrialist eventually went upstairs to write the check.

After he had left the room, Moody began to lament that he had not asked for twice the amount. Throwing himself upon his knees, he began to beseech the Lord for $2,000 from McCormick. After a slight delay, the millionaire returned with a sealed envelope.

Following brief but profuse thanks, Moody rushed from the magnificent mansion to the humble study of a Chicago clergyman, Rev. W. Harsha. Bursting into the preacher's presence, Moody shouted: "Open this! Open it! There is a check for $2,000 inside!"

"How do you know? Have you seen it? Did someone tell you?"

"No," said Moody. "But I asked the Lord for it, and I have come all the way across the city to have you open it so that you could prove my faith in prayer."

Moody and Harsha's son stood beside the minister as he ripped open the envelope and pulled out a check payable to

Moody—in the amount of $2,000!

Later McCormick told Harsha he had retired to his room to write the check, had gotten as far as writing the name "D. L. MOODY" as the beneficiary, and then stopped. He began to muse on what a fine man Moody was and what a great work he was doing for Christ in Chicago, then felt strongly impressed to make the check for twice the amount he had originally intended.

Near the end of his ministry, again in Chicago, Moody was praying alone in his room when he realized he needed $3,000 to pay some current bills. He told the Lord he had been so busy with His work he hadn't had time to go out after the money. So he said: "I leave it up to You to send the money in."

That afternoon, during a service, someone slipped an envelope into his hand. Later, when he opened it, he found a check in the exact amount of $3,000. When he called the donor to thank her for the gift, she said that she had started to write it for $2,000, but had been so strongly impressed to increase it that she had.

The donor, by the way, was Mrs. Cyrus H. McCormick!

4. THE POEM:

> **O dumb, deaf, blind, receive!**
> **Shall He who made the ear not hear your cry?**
> **Doth He not tenderly see who made the eye?**
> **Ask Me that I may give.**
>
> —*Adeline D. T. Whitney*

94.

1. THE PROMISE: *"These things have I written unto you that believe on the name of the Son of God; that ye may know that ye have eternal life, and that ye may believe on the name of the Son of God"* (I John 5:13).

2. THE POINT: God has put His infallible Word in writing so that men might believe in His dear Son and, believing, know

with positive assurance that eternal life is theirs.

3. THE PROOF: F. E. Marsh tells of a poor woman in Scotland who attended some evangelistic meetings in Glasgow, conducted by Major D. W. Whittle, an associate of D. L. Moody. On the invitation, the lady went to the inquiry room and trusted her soul to Christ on the basis of our Lord's word in John 5:24: "Verily, verily, I say unto you, He that heareth my word, and believeth on him that sent me, hath everlasting life, and shall not come into condemnation; but is passed from death unto life." Whittle took a little card and wrote the words of the promise on it, then gave the card to the woman.

The redeemed soul left the meeting rejoicing and her joy was so extreme her small son wanted to know what had happened. Best she could, as a new convert, she explained to him what she had experienced. He, too, received Christ as his Saviour!

However, the following morning the mother awoke in a spirit of doubt and despondency. Gone was the bright joy and the happy countenance. When the boy, Harry, inquired as to the trouble, she replied: "I thought I was saved, but now the feelings are all gone."

Quick as a flash, the lad inquired, "But, Mither, has the verse changed?"

Running to the Bible where his mother had placed the card, he got it out, looked at it, then radiantly declared: "No, Mither; it's just the same." Next he turned to the Bible itself, looked up the verse and read it, then ran shouting to his mother, "It's a' here, Mither, the verse is just the same!" And so it was!

4. THE POEM:
>It fortifies my soul to know
>That, though I perish, Truth is so:
>That, howsoe'er I stay and range,
>Whate'er I do, Thou dost not change:
>I steadier step when I recall
>That, if I slip, Thou dost not fall.
>
>*—Arthur Hugh Clough* (1819-1861)

95.

1. THE PROMISE: *"And this is the confidence that we have in him, that, if we ask any thing according to his will, he heareth us: And if we know that he hear us, whatsoever we ask, we know that we have the petitions that we desired of him"* (I John 5:14,15).

2. THE POINT: Confidence in prayer comes through praying in the will of God. The child of God, so doing, can pray through until sweet assurance floods his soul that he "has the petition" he desired of God.

3. THE PROOF: In the summer of 1849, when James Hudson Taylor—later to serve a lifetime in China, where he founded the China Inland Mission—was a lad of seventeen tender years, he picked up a gospel booklet, planning to while away the long hours of an idle afternoon. He intended, he later revealed, only to read the story with which the booklet began, setting it aside whenever the moral or sermon started.

In the meantime, some seventy or eighty miles away, Taylor's mother arose from the dinner table where she was visiting, feeling a special burden to pray for her dear son's conversion to Christ. Locking herself in her room, she determined to stay on her knees until assured of victory. Hour after hour sped by while she travailed in agonizing intercession. At length assurance of victory came to her heart and the intercession changed to shouts of praise.

Back at home, young Taylor had become so engrossed in the booklet that he forgot to lay it aside when the application commenced. A phrase, "The finished work of Christ," caught his attention and after sober reflection upon its meaning, he dropped to his knees and claimed the Saviour as his very own. Later, after making her promise not to tell, the young convert told his sister what had happened.

About two weeks later, when his mother returned home, he happily met her at the door and declared he had wonderful news. Describing the scene later, he wrote: "I can almost feel that dear mother's arms around my neck, as she pressed me to her bosom and said, 'I know, my boy; I have been rejoicing for a fortnight in the glad tidings you have to tell me.'

" 'Why,' I asked in surprise, 'has Amelia broken her promise? She said she would tell no one.'

"My dear mother assured me that it was not from any human source that she had learned the tidings, and went on to tell the little incident mentioned above. You will agree with me that it would be strange indeed if I were not a believer in the power of prayer.

"Nor was this all. Some little time after, I picked up a pocket book exactly like my own, and thinking it was mine, opened it. The lines that caught my eye were an entry in the little diary, which belonged to my sister, to the effect that she would give herself daily to prayer until God should answer in the conversion of her brother. Exactly one month later the Lord was pleased to turn me from darkness to light."

4. THE POEM:

Prayer is the mightiest force that men can wield;
A power to which Omnipotence doth yield;
A privilege unparalleled, a way
Whereby the Almighty Father can display
His interest in His children's need and care.
Jehovah's storehouse is unlocked by prayer,
And faith doth turn the key. Oh, would that men
Made full proof of this wondrous means, for then
Would mightier blessings on the church be showered,
Her witness owned, her ministers empowered,
And souls ingathered. Then the Gospel's sound
Would soon be heard to earth's remotest bound.

Personality Index

Individual   *Promise*

Individual	Promise
Adlard, Marianne	Psalm 119:149
Austin, "Mother"	Psalm 37:3
Ball, Herman	Romans 14:7
Barnhouse, Donald Grey	II Peter 1:3,4
Baron, David	Romans 12:19
Bingham, Helen E.	Jeremiah 33:3
Bonner, Arthur	II Corinthians 5:17
Boyd, John	Psalm 27:8-10
Bradlaugh, Charles	I Corinthians 2:12,13,15,16
Bray, Billy	Job 12:7-10
———	Proverbs 19:17
Brookes, James H.	Luke 12:6,7
Brooks, Keith L.	Matthew 10:29-31
Brown, John	Joel 2:12,13
Brown, "Rowdy"	II Corinthians 5:17
Bunyan, John	Psalm 23:4
Calvin, John	Psalm 23:4
Cartwright, Peter	I Thessalonians 2:13
———	I Thessalonians 5:24
Chambers, Oswald	Psalm 41:1
———	Psalm 84:5-7
Chapman, J. Wilbur	John 14:1-3
Cheo-Han	Psalm 33:10
Clary, Abel	Isaiah 57:15
Clement of Alexandria	I Peter 4:8
Colgate, William	Psalm 112:1-3
Criswell, W. A.	Mark 11:24
Dixon, A. C.	Psalm 34:15
———	Psalm 145:18,19
Dyer, Maria	Matthew 6:28-30

Finney, Charles G.	Psalm 37:3
————	Isaiah 57:15
————	John 15:7
————	James 5:16
Fuller, Charles E.	Ephesians 1:18
Gardner, Newport	James 2:5
Goforth, Jonathan	Proverbs 3:5,6
	Philippians 4:19
Goforth, Rosalind	Proverbs 3:5,6
————	Philippians 4:19
Goodwin, Mrs. Sally	Psalm 50:14,15
Gordon, Adoniram Judson	Psalm 112:1-3
————	Proverbs 22:9
Gordon, S. D.	John 15:7
Gutzlaff, Charles	Psalm 37:23
Haldeman, William	James 1:5
Hall, Gordon	Psalm 76:10
Hall, Robert	John 14:1-3
Harms, Louis	John 1:50
Harvey, Paul	Nahum 1:3
Harvey, Richard H.	Matthew 17:20,21
Hopkins, Samuel	James 2:5
Hutchens, Paul	Psalm 16:7
————	II Corinthians 12:9,10
Ingersoll, Bob	I Corinthians 2:12,13,15,16
"Jimmy the Rat"	Hebrews 7:25
John, the Apostle	I Peter 4:8
Johnson, R. K. "Lefty"	Proverbs 20:24
Jones, Bob	Proverbs 20:24
Judson, Adoniram	Psalm 76:10
————	Hebrews 4:15,16
LaFontaine, Chaplain	I Corinthians 10:13
Lee, Robert G.	Psalm 50:14,15
Lessy, Rev.	Psalm 119:149
LeTourneau, Robert Gilmour	I Samuel 2:30
Lincoln, Abraham	I Thessalonians 2:13

Livingstone, David	Psalm 37:23
Loest, Daniel	Psalm 38:15,16
Luther, Martin	Psalm 23:4
Marsh, F. E.	I John 5:13
Martyn, Henry	Psalm 37:23
McAuley, Jerry	II Corinthians 5:17
McBeth, Leon	Mark 11:24
McCormick, Cyrus H.	I John 3:21,22
Mills, Samuel	Psalm 76:10
Moffat, Robert	Psalm 37:23
Moody, Dwight Lyman	Psalm 23:4
————	Psalm 84:11
————	Psalm 119:149
————	Jeremiah 23:29
————	Hebrews 6:10
————	I John 3:21,22
————	I John 5:13
Moody, William R.	Psalm 119:149
Moorhouse, Henry	Psalm 11:7
Morgan, G. Campbell	Psalm 119:149
————	I Corinthians 2:12,13,15,16
Muller, George	Matthew 6:34
————	Romans 14:7
	I Peter 3:1,2
Murray, Andrew	I Timothy 1:15
Paton, John Gibson	Psalm 91:5
————	Luke 10:18,19
Paulus, Beate	Psalm 9:9,10
Pierson, Arthur T.	Hebrews 4:12,13
Preston, "Holy Ann"	Jeremiah 33:3
Quarterman, John	Matthew 6:28-30
Rainier, Peter W.	Psalm 46:8-10
Rice, John R.	Jeremiah 29:11-13
	Matthew 18:19,20
————	Galatians 6:8,9
Rice, Luther	Psalm 76:10

Rice, Will	Galatians 6:8,9
Richards, James	Psalm 76:10
Rimmer, Harry	Colossians 1:6
Rommel, Gen. Erwin	Psalm 46:8-10
Rutherford, Samuel	Philippians 1:21,23
Smith, Gipsy	Ezekiel 11:19,20
————	I John 2:29
Smith, James H.	I Peter 5:7
Smith, Nicholas	Psalm 61:3,4
Spurgeon, Charles Haddon	Psalm 41:4
————	Psalm 145:18,19
Stuart, George	Proverbs 22:15
Sumner, Robert L.	John 1:12
Sumer, Mrs. Robert L.	Psalm 86:6,7
Sumner, Ron	Psalm 86:6,7
Sunday, Billy	Psalm 19:1-4b, 7-11
————	Proverbs 28:13
Tam, Stanley	Psalm 143:8
Tate, Bill	Matthew 6:33
Taylor, J. Hudson	Matthew 6:28-30
————	Luke 6:30,38
————	Luke 12:6,7
————	John 4:13,14
	I John 5:14,15
Toplady, Augustus Montague	Psalm 23:4
Torrey, Rueben Archer	Hebrews 6:10
Trumbull, Henry Clay	John 14:13,14
Truett, George W.	II Corinthians 1:3,4
Twitchell, J. H.	Mark 1:17
Uxhill, Baron	Hebrews 4:12,13
Vassar, "Uncle John"	Psalm 121:7,8
————	Mark 1:17
Veal, Mrs. Minnie Slaughter	Mark 11:24
Voltaire (Francois Marie Arouet)	Psalm 33:10
Von Kottwitz, Baron	Psalm 38:15,16
Wesley, John	Psalm 23:4

Whittle, Major D. W.   I John 5:13
Wilberforce, Bishop Samuel   John 14:1-3

Poet Index

Author   *Promise*

St. Anatolius, Bishop of
   Constantinople   Ezekiel 11:19,20

Bathurst, William H.   Psalm 143:8
Bonar, Horatius   Colossians 1:6
Bliss, Philip Paul   Matthew 17:20,21
Buell, Harriett Eugenia Peck   Ephesians 1:18
Burns, James Drummond   Psalm 50:14,15
Burton, John   Jeremiah 29:11-13

Cary, Alice   I John 2:29
Charles, Elizabeth Rundle   Proverbs 22:9
Christiansen, Avis Marguerite
   Burgeson   Psalm 8:2
Clough, Arthur Hugh   I John 5:13
Coleridge, David Hartley   Psalm 86:6,7
Cooke, Rose Terry   Psalm 112:1-3
Cowper, William   Jeremiah 23:29
                                          I Peter 3:1,2
_____
Crosby, Fanny J.   John 14:1-3

Daunecker, Marian N.   Psalm 23:4

Faber, Archbishop Frederick
   William   Luke 10:18,19
Fenelon, Archbishop Francois
   de Salignac de la Mothe   Philippians 1:21,23
Flemming, Paul   Matthew 6:33
Flint, Annie Johnson   Matthew 10:29-31

Gerhardt, Paul	James 2:5
————	II Peter 1:3,4
Gray, James Martin	John 1:12
————	Hebrews 4:12,13
Guyon, Madam Jeanne Marie Bouvier de la Motte	John 4:13,14
Hamilton, Robert B.	II Corinthians 1:3,4
Harris, C. W.	Proverbs 20:24
Harris, Gale	Mark 11:24
Harvey, Bill	Galatians 6:8,9
Havergal, Frances Ridley	I Samuel 2:30
————	Psalm 84:5-7
————	Psalm 84:11
————	Romans 14:7
————	I Thessalonians 5:24
Heber, Bishop Reginald	John 1:50
Ken, Bishop Thomas	James 1:5
Lillenas, Haldor	Psalm 33:10
Logan, John	Jeremiah 33:3
Longfellow, Henry Wadsworth	Psalm 27:8-10
Luther, Martin	Matthew 18:19,20
Lyte, Henry F.	Psalm 91:3,5
McCarthy, Dennis	Psalm 41:1
Midlane, Alfred	Isaiah 57:15
Neumark, Georg	Psalm 38:15,16
Nicholson, James	II Corinthians 5:17
Nicholson, Martha Snell	Hebrews 4:15,16
Pastnor, Paul	Hebrews 13:5,6
Pollard, Adelaide Addison	John 15:7
Proctor, Adelaide Anne	Psalm 16:7
Quarles, Francis	Psalm 9:9,10
Reitz, Albert Simpson	Psalm 34:15
Rossetti, Christina Georgina	Psalm 119:149

Ryberg, Barbara C.	Matthew 6:34
Schlipf, B.	Philippians 4:19
Scott, Sir Walter	Psalm 46:8-10
Scriven, Joseph	John 14:13,14
Simpson, Albert B.	I Corinthians 2:12,13,15,16
Source Unknown	Psalm 11:7
————	Psalm 76:10
————	Psalm 127:7,8
————	Psalm 145:14-16
————	Proverbs 3:5,6
————	Proverbs 16:3
————	Proverbs 19:17
————	Proverbs 22:15
————	Isaiah 26:3,4
————	Mark 1:17
————	Luke 6:30,38
————	Luke 12:6,7
————	Luke 12:24
————	Romans 8:28
————	Romans 12:19
————	I Corinthians 10:13
————	II Corinthians 12:9,10
————	I Thessalonians 2:13
————	I Timothy 1:5
————	Hebrews 6:10
————	Hebrews 7:25
————	I Peter 4:8
————	I Peter 5:7
————	I John 5:14,15
Sumner, Robert L.	Malachi 3:10
Sutton, Henry Septimus	Job 12:7-10
Tennyson, Alfred	Psalm 145:18,19
————	James 5:16
Thaxter, Celia	Psalm 37:23
Trench, Archbishop Richard Chenevix	Joel 2:12,13
Watts, Isaac	Nahum 1:3

Welsh, Robert Gilbert   Matthew 6:28-30
Wesley, Charles   Psalm 61:3,4
————   Proverbs 28:13
Whitney, Adeline D. T.   I John 3:21,22
Whittier, John Greenleaf   Psalm 19:1-4b, 7-11
Williams, Isaac   Psalm 37:3

Other Books by Dr. Sumner

ARMSTRONGISM

Some of the most influential and greatly-used leaders in Christendom have highly commended this authoritative study of Herbert and Garner Ted Armstrong's evil cult. For example, consider some of the following:

". . . detailed, thorough, and comprehensive. It will do much good . . . May God give it wide circulation."

—*Dr. Jack Hyles*

"We recommend this scholarly and important big book. It is true to the Scriptures, and it will be a tremendous revelation to honest readers."

—*Dr. John R. Rice*

". . . an excellent volume! . . . will result in opening the eyes of many . . . I am in hearty agreement with you . . ."

—*Dr. Lee Roberson*

"I am now happy to recommend this book which will answer every question concerning the false teachings of both Herbert and Garner Ted Armstrong."

—*Dr. Jack Van Impe*

". . . well written, well documented, thorough, even kind."

—*Dr. Bob Moore*

". . the largest, the most informative and the most comprehensive book on the American-based cult . . ."

—*Dr. G. Archer Weniger*

". . . very large and detailed book . . . a masterpiece."

—*Dr. Tom Wallace*

"The most documented, thorough examination and expose' of any cult I have ever read . . . superb and extremely helpful . . . a classic work on one of the most insidious cults of our time and should be read by all pastors and Christian workers."

—*Dr. C. Sumner Wemp*

". . . the finest of this type written . . . clear and scholarly . . . honest, sincere, factual and documented . . . God's answer to one of the greatest religious deceptions of all time. It ought to be in every Christian home, in the library of every Bible-believing preacher and in every fundamental college. I am extremely proud to possess a copy of my own."

—*Dr. Tom Malone, Sr.*

ONLY $5.95

15 Chapters, 424 Pages

Hell Is No Joke

This is a book of six strong evangelistic messages dealing with the subjects, *Hell Is No Joke, The Unmocked God, Slipping into Hell, Have You Counted the Cost? Do You Think You Will Go to Heaven When You Die?* and, *Heaven: Home, Sweet Home, of God's Children.* The Pathway Book Club, in offering it as its main monthly selection, said of it: *"The messages are Bible-centered, easy to understand, and are made vivid through the use of interesting illustrations. Each of these messages should provide the reader with a number of 'sermon starters' or add to one's materials for sermon building."*

Reviewers Say:

"We cannot recommend too strongly that every home possible should own this book. These sermons will inspire and start fires burning and give suggestions and illustrations and outlines for preachers. They are full of Bible truth, heart-warming illustrations. They read easily and leave a lasting impact.

"A wonderful way to win souls would be to buy this book and lend it among unsaved friends, in each case pressing the matter of salvation after one had read these sermons."—*The Sword of the Lord.*

"Six evangelistic sermons on Hell, judgment and Heaven by a widely-known evangelist. The messages are expository, clear in outline, rich in illustration and make a strong appeal for the reader or hearer to turn to God."—*Baptist Record.*

"Plain, pointed and practical preaching here! While the themes are as old as time itself, there are no platitudes here. 'Old-fashioned' preaching that rebukes sin and exalts the Lord."—Dr. Robert Lee Braden, Phoenix, Arizona.

"Here are six typical Sumner sermons, pungent, succinct, Scriptural and evangelistic."—*Baptist Bulletin.*

"This book of six sermons carries the same sober urgency suggested in the title. As in any of Sumner's works, the material is clearly marked by those attributes which equip him for his multifarious duties... Mr. Sumner has a presentation of pathos and force. The messages are bibliocentric and worthy of a place in your library."—*Baptist Bible Tribune.*

"... a great warning to men of the danger that confronts them who neglect the Word of the Lord and the salvation He has provided... It should be read with great and careful interest by both saint and sinner. Its warnings are very timely and essentially needful."—*The Ohio Independent Baptist.*

$3.25

5 for $15.00
10 for $28.00

Biblical Evangelism In Action!

"... ONE OF THE MOST HELPFUL BOOKS ON SOUL WINNING TO APPEAR IN THIS GENERATION ... LOADED WITH WORKABLE IDEAS ... BEARS OUR UNCONDITIONAL RECOMMENDATION."
—Dr. G. Archer Weniger

"We do not know of any book similar in nature which is as practical and thorough."—THE BAPTIST BULLETIN

"HOW I REJOICE IN THE APPEARANCE UPON THE STAGE OF CHRISTIAN LITERATURE OF THIS GREAT BOOK ..."
—Dr. Tom Malone, President, Midwestern Baptist College; Pastor, Immanuel Baptist Church, Pontiac, Michigan.

"I WOULD LIKE TO GIVE MY FULL COMMENDATION ... IT IS INTERESTING READING AND CONVINCING IN ITS PRESENTATION ..."
—Dr. Lee Roberson, Chancellor, Tennessee Temple Schools; Pastor, Highland Park Baptist Church, Chattanooga, Tennessee.

Only $5.50

EVANGELISM: The Church on Fire

This book comprises a series of ten lectures on evangelism delivered by the author at the Grand Rapids Baptist Bible College & Seminary. The publishers have summed up this significant volume with the words: *"In forceful, practical, stimulating style, Mr. Sumner describes the need for New Testament evangelism, the meaning of New Testament evangelism, personal and pulpit qualifications of New Testament evangelists, regular and special evangelism in the New Testament church, evangelistic preaching, good manners in evangelism, and conserving the results of evangelism."*

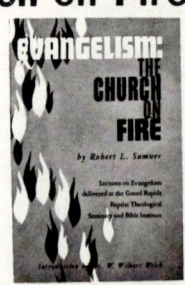

"... a very challenging book. My own desire to win the lost was intensified by reading it."—Dr. John G. Balyo, Cedar Hill Baptist Church, Cleveland, Ohio.

"Several features make this one of the most important books written on evangelism in the last twenty-five or more years."
—Evangelist John R. Rice.

220 Pages

$2.95

"... if churches ever need a book like this and the message it contains, the time is now!"—Dr. Walt Handford, Southside Baptist Church, Greenville, South Carolina.

The Book EVERYONE Is Talking About!

THE MENACE OF NARCOTICS!
by Dr. Robert L. Sumner

"... combines the fervor of an evangelist, the compassion of a pastor, the depth of a theologian, and the love of a father to warn our youth ... a must for every parent, teen-ager and child."
—*Dr. Jack Hyles*, First Baptist, Hammond

"... a 'must' book for the public in general and for the Christian in particular ... This author has done an excellent job ..."
—*Information Bulletin,*
FUNDAMENTAL BAPTIST FELLOWSHIP

"... should be considered a must for parents, teens, pastors, Sunday school teachers and youth workers."
—*Ohio Independent Baptist*

"... a valuable contribution to the libraries of pastors and youth workers."
—*Dr. Bob Moore*, Marietta Baptist Tabernacle

"... quite possibly the best treatment on this subject ..."
—*Dr. G. Archer Weniger*, THE BLU-PRINT

"... a tremendous work. The tips to parents and advice to victims is worth any price."
—*Dr. Tom Wallace*, In THE BEAM

"... A very practical book ... certainly needed today ... well-written, well-illustrated, and true to the Bible ... should have a very wide circulation."
—*Christian Victory*

"... informative, compelling, activating, alarming and convincing. We highly recommend its wide circulation ..."
—*The Sword of the Lord*

"... hard-hitting, clear, documented ... Use it for reference. Read it for facts ..."
—*The Bible for Today*

"... a good, inexpensive book ... needs to be read by every fundamental believer."
—*The Baptist Bulletin*

"An excellent book ... discusses the drug problem frankly and intelligently ..."
—*Grace and Life*

ONLY $1.95
(Plus .50 Postage and Handling)

"... should be demanded coursebook for every school—Grade School through Post Graduate University—and the students should be made to take an examination in it."
—*Dr. Hyman Appelman*, Noted Jewish Evangelist